Start Your Own

CLOTHING STORE AND MORE

Additional titles in *Entrepreneur's **Startup Series***

Start Your Own

Entrepreneur
MAGAZINE'S

startup

2ND EDITION

Start Your Own

CLOTHING STORE AND MORE

Childrens • Bridal
Vintage • Consignment

Entrepreneur Press and Charlene Davis

Ep
Entrepreneur
Press

Editorial Director: Jere L. Calmes
Managing Editor: Marla Markman
Cover Design: Beth Hansen-Winter
Production and Composition: Eliot House Productions

This publication is designed to provide accurate and authoritative information in regard to the subject matter covered. It is sold with the understanding that the publisher is not engaged in rendering legal, accounting or other professional services. If legal advice or other expert assistance is required, the services of a competent professional person should be sought.

Library of Congress Cataloging-in-Publication Data
Davis, Charlene, 1957–
   Start your own clothing store and more/by Entrepreneur Press and Charlene Davis.—2nd ed.
     p.   cm.
   Rev. ed. of: Start your own clothing store/Julie Miller. c2003.
   Includes index.
   ISBN-13: 978-1-59918-125-7 (alk. paper)
   ISBN-10: 1-59918-125-8 (alk. paper)
   1. Clothing trade—Management. 2. Stores, Retail—Management. 3. New business enterprises—Management. I. Miller, Julie. Start your own clothing store. II. Entrepreneur Press. III. Title.

HD9940.A2M55 2007
687.068'1—dc22   2007011670

Printed in United States of America
12 11 10 09 08   10 9 8 7 6 5 4 3 2 1

Contents

▲

Chapter 12

Chapter 13

Preface

The *Start Your Own Clothing Store* book is written for the fashion-conscious individual with an acute sense of business. Although anyone can open a clothing retail store—especially after reading this book—it is not for the faint of heart. It requires dedication, long hours, experience in the fashion industry—and some cash. Whether a fashion-savvy entrepreneur wants to build a clothing empire or settle comfortably in a small boutique, this book will lay the groundwork from beginning to end.

Readers will learn how to spot new trends and forecast upcoming styles, while analyzing their competition and getting the jump on them. Although doing homework is generally not fun, entrepreneurs will enjoy sizing up the market while studying demographics and locating the right site. They will also learn the mechanics of setting up their store to its best advantage while creatively displaying their wares. In addition to exhibiting the apparel, entrepreneurs will also learn how to effectively find, track, stock, and store their inventory.

Once readers know what to sell and where to sell it, they will then learn *how* to sell it using a myriad of marketing strategies. Also, hired help is usually a must and there is an art to successfully hiring, firing, and training employees, which will be discussed in detail.

Most importantly, finding a niche or specialty is the key to success, and this book will discuss several different concepts including how to cater to women, men, or children, developing their own brand, reselling vintage and consignment wear, or opening a specialty boutique.

The fashion industry is always going to be in vogue, and with courage, talent, and resources, a clothing store entrepreneur can be well on their way to success!

Introduction
The Apparel Entrepreneur

"Shop 'til you drop." It's arguably one of America's favorite mantras, whether we're stocking up on Nikes, spandex, or low-rise jeans.

Whether you're a Prada poseur or a Dockers devotee, chances are you know all about fashion obsessions (More heels than Carrie Bradshaw in *Sex and the City*? More sneakers than Jerry Seinfeld?) and can drop names like Miyake or Manolo at the drop of a feather boa. And if you're interested in opening your own apparel store, chances are you may not own a feather boa, but you're probably aware of the kind of money savvy apparel entrepreneurs can make if they know their market. What do you think of when you hear mention of the Gap or Gymboree?

During the 1990s, the apparel industry experienced a bit of a slowdown as consumers turned their attention away from clothes toward electronics. However, that trend re-shifted after electronics and computer-related equipment suffered a sharp decline in 2005. According to MarketResearch.com, that is the year the apparel retail industry generated total revenues of $827 billion worldwide. Forecasts predict that performance sales in this industry will increase by a compound annual growth rate of 2.9 percent for the period of 2005 through 2010. This would culminate in more than $953 billion in total global revenues by the end of 2010. While spending will continue to increase in all retail categories, apparel and electronic purchases will maintain their status as retail leaders of the pack.

It's Not a Fad, Fad, Fad, Fad World

One of the keys to your success as an apparel entrepreneur will be your discerning taste. Having an eye for trends takes more than watching the Style Network or the Academy Awards. The apparel business can be risky—ask the flamboyant Isaac Mizrahi, whose ready-to-wear label went bankrupt in 2004—so if you think you might want to open a women's boutique in a middle-income neighborhood, you'd better be sure you stock more than sequined bustiers and stiletto heels. The point is you are not going to want to stock the same merchandise in suburban Cleveland as you would in lower Manhattan.

Whether you decide to open a store in suburban Cleveland, at the Mall of America, or above a coffee shop in lower Manhattan, you'll have to do your homework. What are people buying in your neck of the woods?

As you will learn in this business guide, the secret to success in the apparel business is location, knowing the tastes of your market, and money—and as you'll also learn, not necessarily in that order. These are the basic ingredients of a profitable store.

This recipe includes other factors as well. How ambitious are you? How adept are you at managing people, many of whom will be working for not much more than minimum wage? Are you willing to work long hours every day and give up your weekends? Do you have strong financial backing or know where to get it? Do you know cotton from chenille, Dolce from Dockers, or Calvin Klein from Charter Club?

Another important factor is having a certain amount of experience in the apparel business. Just because you were smart enough to keep—or too lazy to throw away—your bell bottoms (which just happened to come back in the '90s), that doesn't mean you're a shoe-in in the apparel business. And if you think the "softer side of Sears" advertising campaign has something to do with the Diehard battery, you may be opening the wrong kind of store.

Most important, as you'll learn again and again throughout this business guide, Fashion = Financial Backing. You cannot run a successful apparel store without savings, a bank loan, or a trust fund. Period.

The Fashion Cycle

Talk about discerning taste. When you think about today's apparel customer, think "champagne taste on a beer budget," because even if your customers can afford to splurge on Cristal, chances are they will go for the bubbly before they'll buy a Chanel suit—at least at boutique prices.

According to a recent Global Lifestyle Monitor survey, consumers worldwide browse specific retail stores for selection (45 percent), prices (36 percent), style (22 percent), quality of clothing (22 percent), and ease of shopping (21 percent). However, 77 percent of surveyed shoppers from the United States indicated that price was the top consideration when purchasing clothing. The average consumer today is confident about his or her purchasing power and has every right to be. Apparel industry publications refer to the "new" consumer as prosperous yet frugal, able to afford full price yet waiting for markdowns. If you have ever shopped at an apparel outlet mall, you know what we are talking about. Today's consumers are savvy. The overabundance of retail space and merchandise has taught them well: They don't have to buy it today, they don't have to buy it at full price, and they definitely don't have to buy it where they don't want to.

As indicated above, today's consumer wants value, selection, quality, and convenience. Selection means that you have what consumers want when they want it. Value is the perception, or delusion, of quality for the right price—such as an Armani suit for $500 (dream on big spender). Convenience says that finding the right outfit at the right price will not take more than one short trip, and the parking lot won't be full. And that's where you, the independent apparel store owner, come in.

Fickleness, frugality, trends, selection, value, and convenience are all things that today's apparel entrepreneur must keep in mind when opening a store. That, of course, and always keeping one eye on the competition. And there's plenty of it today, from mega apparel retailers like the Gap and The Limited to popular catalogs like J. Crew and Victoria's Secret to the thousands of outlet malls cropping up across the country. Outlet shopping, in fact, has become so popular that shopping locations are becoming tourist destinations in many American guidebooks. Rome has the Trevi Fountain, and Palm Springs has the Cabazon Outlet Mall. Who says we don't have culture in America?

Stepping Out in Style

Fashion is fun! Maybe not for everyone, but for those of us who get goosebumps when we find that perfect pair of shoes on the fourth markdown, leaf through the fat fall issue of Vogue, or splurge on a cozy cashmere sweater.

Maybe you've worked at one of the big retail chains selling handbags for a year; maybe you spent summers working in your family's clothing store; maybe you've even been lucky enough to inherit the family store. Whatever the reason, we'll get you on your way.

In this business guide, we'll tell you everything you ever wanted to know about the apparel business; by the end, you'll confidently be throwing around terms like "open to buy" and "sell through." We'll also help you determine what you're best suited to be selling—men's, women's, or children's clothing—so that you can carve a niche that works and is profitable.

And believe us, you can find a niche in this business—a business in which looking good never goes out of style.

1

Apparel from (A)scots to (Z)ebra Prints

Maybe the idea of starting an apparel store dawned on you one day as you shopped unsuccessfully for some functional lingerie—well, that may be an oxymoron—or a stylish business suit in a plus size. You went home and groused to your spouse or a friend, who said, "You know, you've always had an eye for clothing and good business sense; you should open your own store," or "You've always spent so much money on clothes. Maybe you should just open your own store and get them for free."

You laughed (hopefully), but you were flattered and remembered those fashion merchandising classes that you took back in college before your parents talked you out of a career in clothes and suggested that you pursue a more serious or safe career. On the other hand, maybe you're heir to your family's apparel business and debating whether to be a rebel and go to law school or give in and take it over.

Whatever your circumstances may be, we can say this about all you apparel store owner wanna-bes: You're highly motivated and hard-working, and you derive great satisfaction from taking risks; maybe you even fancy yourself a famous entrepreneur like Richard Branson (minus the spaceship). Either way, we're not talking about a side gig that you can do at your kitchen table after the kids are in bed or when you have some spare time on the weekend. You're opening an apparel store, and that means hard work and long hours on your feet.

We repeat: Opening an apparel store is serious business. For some, it may mean giving up the safety of your corporate job with its steady income, paid holidays, vacations, and opportunity for advancement. All this, and guaranteed 12- to 14-hour days. On the bright side, you'll be your own boss, make six figures a year, and even see your movie star customers talk to Ryan Seacrest and viewers of *E! Entertainment Television* about the clothes they bought at your store. (Well, we can all dream.)

But you can't bet on either the six figures or the moneyed clients. What you can bet on is this: "Running an apparel store is more than a full-time job," stresses Dr. Nancy Stanforth, associate professor at Kent State University's School of Fashion. "Running an apparel store is something you do all day, every day."

Always Room for More

Fortunately, there is always room for the right kind of apparel store. Although you might not guess it by the number of malls and outlet centers cropping up, we are a nation of mostly small, independent merchants. In fact, most retail stores, and that includes apparel stores, are small, both in size and in sales volume, compared with a Gap or a Charlotte Russe store. The typical apparel store is a small operation, usually run by the owner alone or by a husband-and-wife team.

While small stores lack the resources, purchasing skill, and sophistication of big apparel retailers, such as Banana Republic, studies show that small stores demonstrate surprising resiliency in the face of competition (for a multitude of reasons we'll go into throughout this business guide). At their most successful, they offer consumers convenient locations, more personalized service, a warmer atmosphere and often, a broader selection of merchandise in their particular lines than the larger chain stores. And if you do your homework—and follow the suggestions and expert advice provided by this business guide—there's a chance the store you launch today may become the next Express. Now if that gets your adrenaline pumping, you're shopping in the right department.

> **Smart Tip**
> The keys to success in the apparel business are enough financial backing, the right location, and knowledge of your market.

The Answer Is Absolutely Apparel

We'll presume that your desire to open an apparel store is not because you want to prove to your ex that you're actually hip and happening, or because you are so confident of your style that you need to share that good taste with the community—or even because you have all those fashion merchandising classes under your belt. We'll instead presume that you have an acute business sense, a sincere interest in the clothing business, and more than a little cash in the bank.

According to BizStats.com, clothing and accessories retail stores have approximately a 41 percent chance of failing during the first year. Aside from the obvious factors—lousy location or inadequate financial backing—apparel store owners often have a romanticized notion of their business. They might think if they are a sharp dresser, they should open a clothing store. Then they discover their taste levels don't match their business acumen and in the end, they make better consumers than retailers.

> **Beware!**
> In recent years consumers have moved away from anything associated with traffic and unsecured parking. Shopping/entertainment malls will likely still exist, as consumers are increasingly attracted to safe, secure environments that offer a variety of entertaining options. The bottom line is that leading apparel retailers are doing more to give consumers easy access to a wider range of custom apparel at affordable prices. They are your competition.

Let's not forget that a big part of opening an apparel store is hiring and managing a group of employees, often a young and transient group still in high school or college just looking for part-time work to pay for their prom or pledge formal dresses. We'll delve into this more deeply in Chapter 9, but for now, we just want to play devil's advocate and make sure you know what you're getting into. We've even come up with a handy set of questions that will help you determine whether fashion is indeed your forte.

Experience Desired

OK, this might seem like an obvious question, but you'd be surprised at the number of people out there who think that because they have, well, owned their own tax preparation business, they can open a teen-oriented surf boutique when they have a midlife crisis. Now, we don't mean to pick on tax preparers, and it's certainly been proven that anything is possible—John Glenn went back into space,

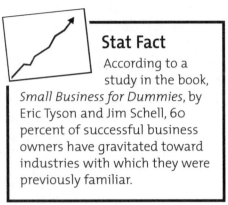

Stat Fact
According to a study in the book, *Small Business for Dummies*, by Eric Tyson and Jim Schell, 60 percent of successful business owners have gravitated toward industries with which they were previously familiar.

didn't he?—but when it comes to clothes, you need to know the "right stuff."

We are not saying that you need a business card laden with a lot of impressive acronyms or a Ph.D. or master's degree—though a master's in business can't hurt an entrepreneurial endeavor. Maybe you've taken those merchandising classes; maybe you've watched your father, mother, or grandparents run a business; maybe you spent a summer selling makeup over the counter at Macy's. In any case, your experience and business sense are as important as your interest in clothes.

How you get the experience is up to you. You may want to take some classes, read books or tap the expertise of a friend or mentor in the business. "The seven years I worked as a buyer for another local clothing store gave me invaluable direction," says Robert Loeb, an apparel store owner in Meridian, Mississippi. "It was the best thing I could have done to ensure the success of my own store."

Risky Business

This is not meant to scare you; we're only trying to present a balanced picture. If you're serious about opening an apparel store, you need to know that the apparel business is risky. You may pour your life savings into a business that goes bust within a year.

Stat Fact
Last year, Americans spent more than $177 billion on filling their closets with clothing, shoes, and accessories, which was up 2.2 percent from the previous year, according to the NPD Group, a Port Washington, New York-based retail research company.

"Nothing is sure-fire, and there are risks attached to starting any kind of business," says Fred Derring, principal of D.L.S. Outfitters, a New York City-based apparel marketing and consulting company, "but you've really got to love the clothing business because you can make more money doing almost anything else. Even in the restaurant business—if you're successful—you can make more money in five years than you can in 15 years in the apparel business."

In fact, let's just lay all the negatives out on the table, so to speak, and get them out of the way. Apparel retailing offers:

- the chance to gamble with your savings—and maybe with borrowed capital, too—with the odds really stacked against you;
- hard work and long hours, often including nights and Saturdays (the busiest day of the week for many apparel store owners);
- profits measured in pennies on the dollar—when they finally come in; that means eating more dinners at McDonald's than Spago;
- months and months without even a minimum salary, in the majority of cases;
- lots of busywork, like checking off deliveries, putting stock away, housekeeping, ordering merchandise, waiting on customers, lugging cartons, and changing interior and window displays;
- concern over the possibility of shoplifters ripping you off and worry about burglaries.

If your adrenaline is still pumping, good for you.

Clap Your Hands if You Believe

We'll again reference Question No. 1. If you're a CPA who has also been a lifelong surfer, we say go ahead and open that surf boutique. You know the lingo better than any Harvard MBA, and you probably have just the right head for this business. But as we said, if you are opening that leather shop only because during the divorce hearing your wife told the court you were dull and boring, maybe you'd better sit down and figure out if this is the best mode of revenge.

On a serious note, you really need to think about why you've decided to open an apparel store vs. a homeopathic pharmacy or an organic grocery store. You may be able to pontificate on the textural qualities of chenille and cashmere. You may notice and appreciate the stylistic differences among Calvin Klein, Donna Karan, and Big Dog. You may know the exact date the new DKNY lines come in to your local Bloomingdale's. Most important, however, you know that a "buy through" is not an open-air garage that sells clothing.

"In my case, I was burned out in the family business when I purchased my first retail store," says apparel store owner and international

> **Tip...**
>
> **Smart Tip**
> Staying current is a biggie, as some veteran apparel companies have come to realize. According to *Newsweek* magazine, the Lands' End product line has grown stale. Says William Dean, a catalog-industry consultant quoted in the magazine, "Their merchandise got tired. There's nothing exciting, nothing new that's going to drive me to buy another blue tennis shirt." Keep excitement in mind when you open your own store.

retail expert, Debbie Allen. "I was business-savvy, but instead of trying to go out on my own, I bought my boutique from my mother in Indiana. I purchased a business that had not turned a profit in six years, but I still saw it as an opportunity to learn the industry and turn the store around. I turned it around and grew the business ten times in just three short years, then opened up two more locations. I built them to a high level of success and then sold them all for full cash price without a business broker. I now share my knowledge of the business industry and my passion for business growth with retailers around the world as a professional speaker and author."

Whatever your passion, it has to be enough to carry you through the yearly holiday rushes as well as the slow summer lulls. It's like marriage. When times get tough, you need to remember why you took those vows in the first place.

Standing Out in the Crowd

It doesn't take a Ph.D. to see that the apparel industry is crowded. All you need to do is save all those catalogs stuffed in your mailbox or visit your local mall on the

---

Getting Government Goods

You can place your trust—yes, we said trust—in the following government organizations:

○ *The Small Business Answer Desk.* This is a free service of the SBA. You can call (800) 827-5722 to speak with a living, breathing SBA employee who will provide you with a thorough list of government resources and referrals, along with all kinds of advice.

○ *Service Corps of Retired Executives (SCORE).* Federally funded, SCORE consists of more than 12,000 nationwide volunteers who provide free counseling and advice to prospective or existing businesses. Know that the majority of SCORE's volunteers are ex-Fortune 500 employees and may not be the best small-business resources. If you happen to be assigned to the right volunteer, however, SCORE can be the best deal in town—occasionally even providing you with that much-needed mentor. Call (800) 634-0425 for the SCORE office near you, or visit its web site at www.score.org.

○ *Office of Business Liaison.* Associated with the Department of Commerce, this agency helps small-business owners locate the federal agency best able to serve their particular needs. Call (202) 482-1360 or visit their web site at www.osec.doc.gov/obl.

---

weekend. But there always seems to be room for more, particularly if you're offering consumers something they feel they're lacking.

And regardless of how successful the Gap, Banana Republic, and Pacific Sun are today, consumers not only mix and match their clothes, they also mix and match their favorite apparel stores, according to K. Cohlmia, owner of a unisex apparel store in Stillwater, Oklahoma. "These days, the look is a lot more eclectic," Cohlmia says. "For example, you might see a man come in wearing a Barney's New York jacket with an Old Navy T-shirt and Levi's. People really mix fashion up these days, which is great news for the independent store owner."

What's Your Specialty?

When opening an apparel store, you need to have the corner on something someone else in your professional community doesn't. Maybe it's beachwear; maybe it's chic plus-size fashions; maybe it's leather and jewelry imported from Turkey.

More and more, women are looking to specialty retailers in their quest to find cutting-edge apparel that is suitable for different body types, lifestyles, and ages. Growth areas include specialty athletic apparel, maternity wear, footwear, and clothing for over-40s, as well as petite and plus sizes. Market research firm The NPD Group recently reported that loyal customers of upscale retailers buy more than 25 percent of their apparel at high-end stores and spend an average of $95 per shopping trip. Consider the following tips when planning your own specialty clothing store:

- Be realistic about start-up costs—what you have and what you can get; then proceed from there.
- Define your market, whether it's plus-size women or novelty swimwear.
- Sharpen your sales techniques so that your business will be known as the ultimate in customer service.
- Take it to the web by opening an online store to compliment your brick and mortar one.
- Be a problem solver. If a customer has a dilemma help them work it out—even it means sending them to a competitor.

As you'll learn in later chapters, specializing, or finding your niche, is crucial to your success in this business. And in many cases, all it takes is a little common sense. As one apparel buyer from New York City, says, "No apparel store should be stocking twill khaki shorts if there's a Gap within ten miles."

Analyzing the Competition

In a word, this is called "marketing," which we'll cover in detail in Chapter 12. For now, hear this collective quote culled from every apparel entrepreneur interviewed for this business guide: "Today the competition isn't two doors down the block; it's at the local mall. People can get everything we sell at their local mall, so we have to set ourselves apart other ways. Pay attention to the demographics in your area, to the location and available foot traffic, to television and movies, and to what people are wearing on the street."

Trend-Spotting: Know the Buzz

If you want to profit rather than merely break even in the apparel business (and who doesn't?), soak up information like a sponge and read all the *Cliff's Notes* you can. We know this might be hard, but take time to watch television. Now you actually have a good excuse to watch reruns of *Sex and the City* and *Desperate Housewives*. Read apparel magazines and industry trade publications, such as *Apparel Magazine*. Visit clothing marts to spot trends. Read Chapter 11, "Getting the Goods."

Mentoring Matters

If this is a brand-new venture, we strongly advise you to find a mentor—preferably a veteran apparel store owner who will let you pick his or her brain for the price of an occasional lunch or dinner. If you don't know anyone personally, ask your banker, accountant, lawyer, and any other peers who might be wired into the apparel community for names of friendly apparel business store owners. Join the Chamber of Commerce and other networking organizations to meet others who have "been there and done that." There are also mentoring programs available through the internet for just about any type of business.

Keep in mind this is a relationship; you want to make sure that you and your mentor are compatible. Unless you are enlisting an actual friend in the apparel business, the best way to contact your prospective mentor is to write him or her a letter introducing yourself and your business and the reason for your interest. Don't forget to flatter this person. "I've always admired your taste," is a good ice-breaker. Or try, "I've noticed the most fashionable people in town shop in your store." Then follow up the letter with a phone call.

Assure him or her that you are not after any financial backing, money or, for that matter, his or her cell phone number for emergencies. Instead, acknowledge that their time is valuable, and promise not to waste one nanosecond of it. Provide a list of questions ahead of time—and then find out their favorite local eatery!

Understand that mentoring is a personal experience, not a business one. If the chemistry is right, the relationship will work well. If the chemistry doesn't work, the relationship won't work either.

Chic or Chick?

Think you've got fashion sense? Just for fun, see you if you can come up with the right design industry names to match the following initials:

CK   _____

DKNY   _____

CD   _____

CM   _____

EU   _____

RL   _____

GV   _____

G   _____

KL   _____

NR   _____

TM   _____

V   _____

YSL   _____

TH   _____

AW   _____

AK   _____

N   _____

HB   _____

ON   _____

BR   _____

Answers (in descending order): Calvin Klein, Donna Karan New York, Christian Dior, Claude Montana, Emanuel Ungaro, Ralph Lauren, Gianni Versace, Gucci, Karl Lagerfeld, Nina Ricci, Thierry Mugler, Valentino, Yves Saint Laurent, Tommy Hilfiger, Anna Wintour (editor of *Vogue*), Anne Klein, Nike, Hugo Boss, Old Navy, Banana Republic.

Be honest and straightforward about the problems you face in starting your store, whether you're talking about money or tacky fixtures. And don't be afraid to have your ideas shot down. Most mentors prefer to deal with longer-term strategic issues as opposed to the day-to-day (my sales associate leaves early every day to pick up her babysitter). By the same token, don't blindly follow someone else's advice without doing a little research on your own.

Smart Tip

Let your mentor know how much you value their help by sending a thank-you note, gift basket or other token of your appreciation.

The Bare Threads

One last, but certainly not least, important issue: You don't have to own a feather boa or a leather bustier (we promise to come up with some different examples), and we don't expect that you'll be sitting next to fashion icons such as Anna Wintour or David Beckham at the spring and fall shows. But for crying out loud, you can't expect to open an apparel store and impress your customers if you a) dress like a computer geek, b) think Calvin Klein is one of our ex-presidents, and c) have never set foot in an Old Navy store! Forget fashion—this is simply un-American.

But more important than your own fashion sense will be your handle on fashion-speak, so to speak. As they say, if you're going to walk the walk, you'd better talk the talk. So whether you decide to open a women's, men's or children's apparel store, you'll need to dress up your vocabulary with the words listed in the Glossary at the end of this book.

2

The Fickle Female
Women's Apparel Store

There are no ifs, ands, or buts about it: You gotta love clothes. This particularly applies to the women's apparel store owner. Obviously, if you are a female entrepreneur, you already know that we (yes, we) are a fickle gender when it comes to fashion. It makes absolutely no difference that last year we purchased an entirely new wardrobe; it goes without saying that this season we still have nothing to wear. It doesn't matter if we have five little black dresses (LBDs) hanging in our closet that were collectively worn five times. We simply must have a new LBD for this year's Christmas party, because you never know which person from the office may have seen us at that family wedding (really lame excuse). And it doesn't matter if we have ten pairs of jeans (we really have more). There is always a new pair to buy—and that pair won't fit, either.

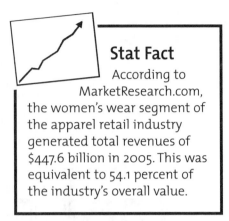

Stat Fact
According to MarketResearch.com, the women's wear segment of the apparel retail industry generated total revenues of $447.6 billion in 2005. This was equivalent to 54.1 percent of the industry's overall value.

Now, if you are a man, or a male apparel store owner, you may not inherently understand this way of thinking. But if you have a spouse, girlfriend, and/or teenage daughters, you are no doubt nodding your head in agreement, if not with slight annoyance! Either way, it's a fairly simple learning curve. As females, we may like an article of clothing today, but we are entitled to change our minds about it tomorrow.

What does this schizophrenia mean for the owner of a women's apparel store? What it means is that to be successful, you need to constantly keep in mind the fickle female psyche—even if you are a man. Men may be from Mars and women from Venus, but when it comes to clothes, we're all better off on the same planet.

"The women's apparel business is exciting because women are more amenable to change and like to try new things," says K. Cohlmia, who owns the Wooden Nickel in Stillwater, Oklahoma. At the same time, most women aren't trendsetters who'd starve themselves or their families to pay for a Dolce & Gabbana sweater set with a faux fur collar. Most, in fact, wouldn't know Dolce & Gabbana from Donny and Marie.

Knowing that, "you don't want to try to be all things to all women and cover everything," says Dr. Nancy Stanforth, associate professor at Kent State University's School of Fashion. "You've got to really focus on your target female customer."

Degrees of Separation

To help you keep focused, let's begin with some more fashion vocabulary specific to the women's market. Styles of women's clothes vary, but essentially you'll be "in the know" if you know the following. There's the traditional look, or preppy style, which features 100 percent natural fabrics like cotton, linen, silk, and wool and often comes in untrendy colors like yellow and lime green. Traditional apparel usually sells well—much better than, say, sweaters with fur collars—particularly now that dressed-down corporate America is as much a reality for women as it is for men.

Basics, which can also be preppy if they're made of natural fibers, are clothes designed more for casual wear and usually contain a good percentage of polyester or synthetic fibers. Basics are popular with a wide cross section of customers because the designs, like sweaters, sweatshirts, and pants with drawstrings or elastic bands, camouflage figure problems. Unless we're lucky enough to be built like Cindy Crawford, we probably all own a few basics.

Fashion items, such as must-have leggings, reflect new trends but are generally the kind of looks that last more than one or two seasons. Updated fashion is trendier and often represents fads like faux fur animal prints, vintage cowboy boots, and low-rise jeans.

Finally, there's designer apparel. All garments with the same designer name have a recognizable look particular to that creator's tastes. American designers like Calvin Klein and Donna Karan, for example, are known for their clean lines and subtle tones, while Tommy Hilfiger's signature bright colors and traditional fabrics might be considered more on the preppy side.

By knowing your target customer, which we'll talk more about in Chapter 12, you'll know which styles to stock. For now, let's just state what might seem like common sense to many of you. In general, lower-income customers will be interested in basics; higher-income customers will go for designer, updated fashions and more traditional styles. A survey of 2,000 women in eight metropolitan areas was conducted by the Associated Merchandising Corporation. Respondents were at least 18 years old, lived in homes with an average income of $35,000, and half worked full time. Sixty-two percent said they buy traditional clothing; 24 percent called their tastes "updated," and 14 percent had "advanced"—fur collars, etc.—tastes.

Cautiously Current

According to experts, this is not an oxymoron in the women's apparel business. One experienced retailer-turned-professional-buyer warns that trying to provide too much variety in style and price can give you a "chop suey" effect, which leaves customers with no fashion direction—not to mention a bank account that is probably equally stirred up. She finds that customers are often disappointed with trends and, in the end, return to safer, more conservative styles. (Remember, we are talking about the "fickle" female.) She believes an apparel retailer's best bet is to offer "newness" more in the form of different colors and fabrics.

Women's Wear Watcher

Prior to starting your store, you can minimize both your financial and fashion risks by following our six-step program in Chapter 1 as well as our passive apparel exercise program of watching TV. Along with that and finding a mentor, you'd be wise to read every book and trade magazine you can find on the specifics of the apparel business—and then watch a little more TV.

Over the years, prime time has played a prime role in women's fashions. Twenty years ago when *Dynasty* was popular, everyone wore gold chokers and football pads on their shoulders. Jump forward 20 years and the new rage was the beaded necklaces inspired by Courteney Cox and Jennifer Aniston of *Friends*. Now it's all about the glamorous little dresses and outfits worn by the *Desperate Housewives* stars. So it's important to pay attention to what women are wearing on TV because those are folks your female consumers want to emulate.

Besides keeping up with changing styles, you should also regularly read magazines and market newsletters to keep up with the values of the clothing and accessories you sell, which we'll discuss more in Chapter 11. As you move on throughout this business guide, you'll see that all of this information will give you ammunition in your discussions with sales reps of the various clothing lines, with whom you'll be doing much negotiating on price and discounts. More important, you will develop an air of authority and an expertise that is important to your professional identity within the industry, and as your business grows, you'll find yourself having to rely less on others' advice.

Smart Tip

Tip...

It's a smart move to subscribe to *Women's Wear Daily* and/or *The New York Times* to keep current on fashion. Also study magazines like *Vogue, Mademoiselle,* and *Glamour.* Read the trades not just for style tips but also for tips on pricing, discounting, and handling and promoting merchandise, which every store manager will be dealing with on a daily basis—and which we'll discuss throughout this business guide.

Sincere Sales Techniques

Everything we've mentioned so far is important; however, the main emphasis of your daily operations as an apparel store owner should be on transforming potential customers into paying customers. This isn't brain surgery; all it takes is common sense and a little sincere encouragement.

Selling involves a "do unto others" mentality, especially where female shoppers are concerned. After all, you know how you don't like to be treated when you are the customer. You don't want to be preyed upon by a hungry stalker. Similarly, as a store owner/salesperson, you want to give each customer sufficient time to browse, after which she may come to you or one of your salespeople with specific questions. Instead of making them feel hunted, make your customers feel at home. Make light conversation. Be attentive and use subtle compliments where appropriate. The longer a customer spends in your store, the more likely you are to make a sale.

Let's take a minute to review the T.O. The term "T.O." stands for "takeover" or "turnover," a psychological technique used to clinch a sale. T.O. works best in a marginal situation. For example, if a customer is lukewarm toward a piece of clothing she doesn't really need but wants, such as platform sneakers decorated with bling. You don't want to use high-pressure tactics, like taking her car keys until she uses her credit card, but if the customer is undecided, it's the perfect opportunity to flip her credit card in your favor.

A Woman's Wish List

In her book, *What Mother Never Told Ya About Retail* (Retail Resources Publications), author T.J. Reid surveyed 2,000 women, ages 21 to 50, in the $30,000 income bracket range, who were asked to rank their shopping desires in order of priority. They were also asked to indicate if they would be willing to pay higher prices if a store provided the extras they wanted. Here are the top "wants":

Wish List	Want	Would Pay Extra for
Restrooms	93%	46%
Places to sit	62%	40%
Delivery	57%	37%
Phone shopping	50%	37%
Coffee/soft drinks	45%	22%
Valet parking	15%	13%

Let's say the customer doesn't respond to the fact that your shoes are tres chic and there's only one pair left in her size. The first thing you need to do, after saying "hello," of course, is to learn what objections the customer has, such as "I'm not sure if the style is flattering" or "I'm not sure whether I'll be able to walk down the street without breaking my neck." Then you or the manager is called in to "take over."

Mind you, this is not a hostile takeover. This is merely a logical sales step for you because you are the fashion authority. You're the owner of this stylish store because you know apparel, right? Use your expertise for all it's worth. Before attempting to counter any objections, begin by subtly and honestly complimenting the customer on her appearance. There need be nothing deceptive about this, unless you ask a woman with gray hair whether she just celebrated her 30th birthday. Honesty is always the best sales technique. Besides, compliments are a kind of support system and most of us use some form of flattery. When it comes to a woman and her clothes, you are simply telling somebody else what she needs to hear.

Get Wise and Accessorize

To accessorize or not to accessorize? It's a viable question when thinking about opening a clothing store and one that, when answered in the affirmative, many seasoned women's apparel store owners say has increased their sales over the years. The thing to remember about accessories is that they require little selling space and create more dollars per square foot than anything else you can offer. Handbags can be hung over garments. Scarves can be tied around collars, and pins displayed on garments.

The trick is also to know what to accessorize with in terms of your market. "I carry a huge variety of jewelry and accessories, like earrings, necklaces, and handbags, many of which are exclusive to my shop in the Savannah area," says Waynette Davenport-Ford, owner of Davenport Designs. "People know when they come in they are not going to find the same merchandise—like the leather purses made by the South African artist, Carrol Boyes—anywhere else in town."

One recent year, apparel store owner and international retail expert, Debbie Allen said that accessories consistently made up 20 percent of her store's sales. Allen says she was selling "tons" of accessories and really worked at up-selling the client with these add-ons. "It does take

Dollar Stretcher

In the beginning, when money is tight and you might not have a good handle on your customers, don't feel that you need to accessorize with the latest, greatest trendy merchandise. It's better to accessorize with low-volume accessories like hosiery, lingerie, and inexpensive costume jewelry.

Accessories: Analyze This

Should you or shouldn't you accessorize your apparel store with accessories? While we say yes, we also want you to be aware of how much you can make on the markup by selling the most sought-after accessories.

Category	Markup
Costume jewelry	53.6%
Scarves	55.0%
Handbags	56.4%
Belts	57.0%
Hair accessories	57.0%
Hosiery	51.3%
Sunglasses	56.0%
Small leather goods	54.3%
Watches	59.0%

focused and frequent buying if you're going to stock and sell accessories," she adds, "because what's popular changes so often."

The NPD Group, a Port Washington, New York, retail research company, reports that handbags are still the most popular accessory purchased by women. "Collecting handbags has become even more important for women today, especially with the new burst of color in fashion," says Marshal Cohen, The NPD Group's chief industry analyst. "Don't be surprised when you hear how many women need to make room in their closet not only for their footwear fetish collection, but their handbag collection as well."

The most popular handbag styles are:

1. Shoulder bag
2. Carry by hand
3. Backpack
4. Sling
5. Messenger Bag
6. Tote Bag
7. Mini bag/Wristlet
8. Clutch

Bright Idea

One or two jewelry cases need to be located within the selling areas, but no definite accessory area should be created. Accessories are impulse items, best merchandised close to the dressing rooms and checkout counters.

Sexy Sports Apparel

This may not seem like the most appropriate chapter in which to be covering sports apparel, but believe it or not, women dominate the sports market, and you might want to include it in your merchandising mix.

According to government data, clothing and accessories sales rose overall by about 3.9 percent; however, sports apparel sales grew by 4.9 percent, according to The NPD Group/NPD Fashionworld. To take advantage of this growing trend, apparel retailers should stay on top of their game by considering the following:

○ Females dominate the decision-making process regarding purchases of sports apparel. Heavy spenders on sports apparel are one-third of all wearers who spend more than 80 percent of all dollars. Guess who the big spenders are: women.

○ According to the Sporting Goods Manufacturers Association (SGMA), women's share of active sports apparel (41.1 percent of dollars spent) is almost equal to men's 42.5 percent share.

○ The SGMA also reports that only 30 percent of all sports apparel actually gets a workout. With multi-function sports clothing expanding its usefulness, the remainder is purchased for casual comfort and leisure wear.

The New York Times reports that 41.3 million American currently hold gym memberships of some sort. So it's no small wonder that Nike focuses on both fashion and function in its products. Women's sports apparel is "a big part of our business, and will continue to grow," said spokeswoman Morgan Shaw. "That includes women's fitness, running, court sports, dance, cardio, and yoga."

It Pays to Play

When designing your women's apparel store, know that women are as apt to change their minds about where they shop as about the kinds of clothes they buy.

Knowing that, you can have some fun. Remember, women come to your store to buy a unique outfit they can't find elsewhere, and their shopping experience should be just as unique.

Depending on your intended customer, whom we'll discuss more in Chapter 12, you have creative license to make your store everything from practical to playful. Whatever you do, keep it feminine. Paint your walls an off-white or pastel, play soft music (if you decide you must have background noise), make sure you have plenty of clothing and accessory displays that change weekly or biweekly, and also offer plenty of comfortable seating. Many women view shopping as a social activity and will often come in with friends or a spouse. Last but not least, keep your store lighting natural or muted.

If you've got something really playful in mind and are worried about cost, take a tip from an apparel store owner who actually arranged to have his store designed by students at a local art school as a class project. By working directly with the instructor, this store owner got his "inside job" done for only the cost of materials.

After reading this chapter we don't expect that you'll be able to read the minds of female shoppers (if you can, be sure to let us know). But a fickle fashion sense can only mean one thing: Women will never stop shopping. And it might as well be at your store.

Macho, Macho Man
Men's Apparel Store

The good news for men is that they don't change their wardrobes every year; they usually rotate a few pairs of favorite jeans, and they don't have the equivalent of a little black dress to obsess about every time there's a social event.

▲

The bad news for owners of men's apparel stores is that men don't change their wardrobes every year; they usually rotate a few pairs of favorite jeans, and they don't have the equivalent of a little black dress to obsess about every time there's a social event.

The trick, then, for the owner of a men's apparel store is not to appeal to a fickle brain (Venus), but one that is mostly functional (Mars), particularly with the growing popularity of dressing down in the increasingly casual workplace.

Cracking the Dress Code

The American workplace is much different than it was a few short years ago, and corporate hiring practices and telecommunications are not the only things that have been affected. With relaxed dress codes now an integral part of more than two-thirds of the workforce, the lines of appropriate business attire have blurred—a lot.

Employees and employers alike (men in particular) are scratching their heads in bewilderment. As K. Cohlmia, from Stillwater, Oklahoma, points out, "While most women thrive on change, extreme fashion for most professional men means an open collar or button-down shirt."

Luckily, extreme is in—apparel insiders refer to it as "business casual," and it's the most prevalent look in menswear today. Clothes may not make the man, but they are certainly making money for apparel store owners who've successfully latched on to the business casual look and beyond.

> **Fun Fact**
>
> How much clout do khakis carry today? One recent summer, Dockers Khakis sponsored San Francisco's Classically Independent Film Festival, with the idea that independent film and the Dockers brand both allow people to express their own sense of personal style.

Barely a decade ago, everyone from seasoned professionals to entry-level clerks knew what appropriate business attire was. "Casual Friday" meant men could remove their ties and don khakis, and women could wear khakis, too. Now the "emerging trend" of the early '90s has evolved into an every day occurrence and the "casual workday" trend has been separated into new categories: business casual, dressy casual, and sports casual. But before you start twitching, we're going to break it down for you:

BUSINESS CASUAL

This is really just a step down from business formal (sans the suit and tie), although ties are optional. This more relaxed look basically consists of a sports jacket in a solid neutral color, or a sweater, paired with coordinating khaki or corduroy slacks. Long-sleeved shirts are the traditional choice, although tucked-in polo shirts (with a sports coat) can be worn for an even more casual look. Nix the jeans, tennis shoes, sandals, shorts, ball caps, T-shirts, and sweatshirts, because they will never be considered business casual.

DRESSY CASUAL

This type of look is what men should feel comfortable wearing to lunch or dinner at a country club or while hobnobbing in the Hamptons. It's also appropriate for a party at a friend's home or dinner at a nice restaurant. A dressy casual ensemble usually pairs open collared shirts with nice slacks; jacket and tie are optional. It looks a lot like business casual attire, with the flexibility to be a tad more casual.

SPORTS CASUAL

The rugged, outdoor look is the most casual look of all and may be suitable for some business and social functions—like meeting friends at the local pub after work or going to a Magic basketball game with the boss (or a date). Denim jeans, polo shirts, and athletic shoes are acceptable; however, T-shirts and ball caps are not.

Since the late-'80s when Casual Friday made its first debut, apparel stores focused on the business casual look have taken a large bite out of the men's apparel industry by specializing in the sale of designer slacks, khakis, and sport shirts rather than traditional suits and ties. While the business casual look has not completely dominated men's fashion—you still see men wearing suits on Wall Street, for instance—the trend has pretty much spread from Silicon Valley to most areas of the country.

Casually Confident

We're going to go out on a limb here and say that casual may go out someday, but it probably won't happen any time soon. To reinforce our millennium mind-set, check out:

- *Brooks Brothers Online (www.brooksbrothers.com).* This famous clothier combines classic elements for all types of dress codes, including custom-made shirts, chinos, and loose-fitting sweaters.
- *Dockers Online (www.dockers.com).* This is the place for khaki, khaki, and more khaki.
- *JoS A. Bank Clothiers (www.josbank.com).* A leader in men's clothing for the workplace that also features a wrinkle-resistant traveler's collection.

▲

But is the business casual look here to stay? Industry insiders seem to think so—at least for the time being. Lois Huff, an analyst at Retail Forward in Columbus, Ohio, was recently quoted in the *Pittsburgh Tribune Review* as saying, "The work uniform of American men is decidedly casual compared to what it was a decade ago." She affirms that, "There's a revived interest in a more structured look, a more tailored look. It's slowing that movement toward the casual, but the casual is still happening."

This doesn't mean you should put the skids on that truckload of new Lacoste polo shirts,

> ## Fun Fact
>
> In 2005, *The New York Times* reported that Donald Trump had beat out and "trumped" Giorgio Armani and Donna Karan as one of the most trusted fashion names in America. That's a pretty good gig for someone who doesn't design, make, promote, or even wear his own line of clothing.

but it does suggest you should be ready to roll with the waves of change. Remember, if we had looked into our crystal ball in the 1970s, we would have seen that disco wouldn't last. "When men wore leisure suits in the '70s, no one thought they'd never have to carry a double-breasted suit again," says Meridian, Mississippi, apparel store owner Robert Loeb. "Then the '80s came along and the leisure suit disappeared. The same thing might happen to business casual, and that's why you have to keep on top of things."

Although business casual gives all appearances of hanging around for a while, the level of casualness depends on your geographic locale and clientele. On the West coast, polo shirts and chinos are a mainstay; but in urban areas such as New York and Chicago, the pendulum is swinging back to a more traditional look that underscores the importance of owning a tie—several, in fact.

Believe it or not—men also pick up certain fashion cues from TV, movies, and men who make millions in other ways, like Miami Heat's head coach, Pat Riley. After all, we had *Miami Vice* to thank for pastel shades and linen suits in the '80s—and certainly those grungy internet entrepreneurs for the less corporate look of the '90s. But since the demise of most of the dot-com businesses, business casual is reviving a more traditional look.

It's probably safe to categorize men's apparel as functional with a flair—a result of corporate trends, nagging spouses, and yes, even vanity tips picked up from studly media figures like Pat Riley and NBC's *Today* show host, Matt Lauer. As one specialty store owner explains, "It used to be that a man would come in and pull a suit off the rack. He had a choice of brown, black, blue, or charcoal. That was it. But in the '80s and '90s men started to become as vain as women, and with that increased vanity came a new awareness of clothing."

Well, frivolous socks and open-mindedness about pink shirts do not a slave to fashion make. Despite the growth of the men's apparel business—and unless you're catering exclusively to those in a creative business like advertising or architecture—you won't find the average computer programmer or Ford executive buying linen suits in pastels or any other color. Remember, most men still suffer from fad-phobia.

Monitoring the Male Mindset

Not to sound like a broken record, but prior to starting your store, you'd be wise to—along with finding a mentor—read every book and trade magazine you can find on the men's apparel business. Become as familiar as you can with the nuances of the industry and the specifics of the male clientele in your area, and regularly read magazines and industry newsletters to keep up with trends. Don't worry; we will hone in more on the male mind-set later in this chapter and in Chapter 12.

We can't stress the value of hands-on experience enough. "My family's apparel business goes all the way back to 1887," says Loeb. "It started as a women's store and gradually, over the years, became focused on menswear. As a teenager and young adult trying to figure out what career I wanted to pursue, I initially went to work for my father part time. But my father told me that if I wanted to be in the apparel business, I needed to learn from the experts. So I went to work in the training department at Parisian's, a major department store down here. I worked for them nearly eight years as both an assistant manager and buyer, and I can now say that it was the best preparation I could have had for running my own business. I learned about pricing merchandise, as well as the industry lingo and how to work with vendors."

We also can't stress enough the importance of developing some kind of niche, whether you decide to be the trendy store owner that carries Paul Smith or the most casual of clothiers. As Cohlmia says, "When we opened in 1975, the store was pretty much a jeans kind of store, and then we had to make the transition to polyester suits like everyone else. In the '80s, we started to carry oxford cloth shirts and khaki pants and were one of the first stores in the area to carry the Polo brand because the look was so hot on the Oklahoma State University campus." Now the store has gone back to its roots by once more becoming a jeans kind of store—as in premium denim jeans for as much as $250 a pair. "We are continually reinventing ourselves to keep pace with demographics and the people who have the money. So we've gone a little younger with hipper styles and sales are skyrocketing.

"I guess what I've learned over the years is that you have to evolve and keep up with the times. If you're not listening to the customers and making changes—you're gone," Cohlmia asserts. "My look for men has always been more of a traditional casual look, and in the past pretty much geared toward the guy in jeans and golfers. But you can't ride the traditional wave forever, especially now that men have become much more casual in the workplace. You've also got to carry khakis and the newer brands. And now, as more of the population spends money on exotic vacations, we are also carrying more travel and outdoor wear, like North Face clothing. My point is, we will probably have to recycle our merchandise again as trends change."

Macho Means Mucho Money

Don't think that just because men aren't as picky about their clothes that starting a men's apparel store will be any cheaper than opening a women's store.

Essentially, we're recommending that you be equally well-financed, which means that even before you start outfitting your store with clothes and fixtures, you'd be wise to have more than $25,000 to get things up and running.

We'll just repeat what we said in Chapter 2, which includes recommendations from experts and entrepreneurs alike. Dr. Nancy Stanforth, associate professor at Kent State University's School of Fashion, recommends $150,000 to keep your sanity, while some entrepreneurs feel they could stay sane starting a store with $50,000. Debbie Allen, industry speaker and owner of Allen & Associates Consulting, Inc. based out of Scottsdale, Arizona, says you should have $100,000 in inventory for a 1,200- to 1,500-square foot store—the average size of an apparel store. Remember: The more money you have, the better off you'll be.

Fun Fact

Levi Strauss & Co. entered into its first-ever movie promotional deal in conjunction with Metro-Goldwyn-Mayer's March 1999 film *The Mod Squad*. The promotion was unusual in that the San Francisco jeans maker visited the movie's production, then created a new line of Levi's-brand clothing to match the look of the film. The clothes are sold by retailers, Original Levi's Stores, and the Levi's web site. Levi also backed the clothes and the movie with a multimillion-dollar ad campaign.

Flattery Will Get You Nowhere

Given a choice between doing the laundry and going shopping, most men will choose folding clothes. For that matter, given the choice between making a commitment to a woman and shopping, most men would just as soon march down the aisle. When men get depressed, they don't shop; they find sports on television or wash the car.

Knowing that, your sales technique with male customers will be very different from how you deal with female customers. Again, with few exceptions, no man is going to respond favorably to the same kind of flattery as a woman: "I like your outfit," "Where do you get your hair cut?" "You look too young to have a child in junior high school," "That shirt looks great with your eyes," etc.

A more effective sales strategy with men is not to flatter them but instead to blur the lines between salesmanship and customer service. Sports is usually a safe topic and a good icebreaker with men. "Did you see the (fill in the blank) game last night?" "How about those (fill in the blank)?" As we said with women, the longer a customer stays in your store, the more likely you are to make a sale.

One thing you don't want to get involved in is the whole T.O. sales method we discussed in Chapter 2. That sort of winning-the-browser-over-to-the-other-side tactic

---

On the Run

If you're a men's apparel store owner whose profits, at least in part, are derived from the sale of athletic shoes, you might be interested in these statistics, gathered from the Sporting Goods Manufacturer's Association (SGMA):

Athletic footwear sales rose 19.3 percent in 2005, with total sales topping $11.96 billion. This was almost $2 billion more than was sold the previous year. The three athletic footwear categories which exceeded the billion dollar mark were:

○ Running/Jogging ($3.15 billion);
○ Basketball ($2.3 billion); and
○ Cross-Training/Fitness ($1.05 billion).

The growth categories in athletic footwear were recreational boots (up 20.7 percent), cross-training/fitness (up 18.8 percent), sport sandals (up 15.6 percent), walking (up 12.2 percent), basketball (up 10.8 percent), running (up 8.9 percent), hiking (up 8.7 percent), aerobic (up 8.5 percent), tennis (up 8.3 percent), and low performance (up 3.5 percent). New categories in the athletic footwear category are cleated ($375 million) and skate/surf ($721 million).

▲

The Minimalist Male

No loud music. No loud colors. No loud accessories. If you don't remember anything else, remember these things when designing your men's apparel store.

As you recall, we're talking about the gender that lists shopping somewhere way below a sporting event and slightly higher than delivering a marriage proposal. That's why you want to make your store as soothing and simple as possible. We'll talk more in Chapter 11 about the current basics of merchandising, but we won't be giving away the store by suggesting here that you keep your men's apparel store low-key and clean.

By low-key, we mean forget any kind of gimmick or theme. If in doubt, paint your walls off-white and leave it at that. By clean, we mean easy to navigate and organized. Place all blazers in one area, all shirts in another, all suits in another. As in a women's store, have plenty of clothing and accessory displays that change regularly. And as we said before, if you're worried about keeping costs down, go straight to the nearest college interior design program.

doesn't work with men, or even their significant others, because if a man or a couple is in your store, they're on a merchandise mission. "When a man walks into your store, you know he wants to buy something," says Loeb. "And usually if the man is there without his wife or girlfriend, it means he's interested in a high-ticket item, like a sports jacket he probably needs for work or some event where she will accompany him and doesn't want to be embarrassed by his clothes. He will go straight to the area of the store where you carry those items and start trying them on. You don't need to worry about following him around to see if you can help him figure out what he needs."

And if you get a man into your store more than once, he might be hooked—at least as much as a man can get hooked on clothes. "You want to make that customer a friend and let him know you'll take care of his needs," says Loeb. "Ask his name; call him by name. Establish a bond by inquiring about his family. Believe me, he'll never get this kind of attention at the Gap."

"I recently had a man in here who told me, 'If you retire, I probably won't ever buy clothes again because I won't know where to go or what to buy. I've gotten so used to you advising me.' You build loyalty and sales by taking care of your customers."

Sports casual or business professional. Venus and Mars. Khakis vs. premium denim. We know this alone is a lot to absorb in a chapter, but hopefully we've provided you with mucho information about the macho man.

4

You've Come a Long Way, Baby
Children's Apparel Store

Maybe it's all those cute clothes at the Baby Gap. Maybe it's your own three kids. Maybe your fashion sense stops at puberty. Any or all of those reasons aren't enough to hang your hat on as a children's apparel store owner, but they're a start. And as we've been hammering home, interest is the number-two qualifier (after money) in this business, whether we're talking Calvin Klein or Carter's.

Running a children's apparel store is different from opening a women's or men's apparel store. One of the most important things to remember is that parents, not children, are the ones with the credit cards and checkbooks. Second, children don't become decades-long customers; their parents do, and then, of course, only if they have more children.

Keeping this in mind, you don't have the option of deciding if the let's-be-friends sales tactic of other apparel stores fits here. We'll tell you now that it does. Running a store that sells items that become obsolete in a month or two because of growth spurts, you'll quickly get to know Megan's or Tommy's mother on a first-name basis. And good thing, too, because hopefully those mothers, and friends, will be back again and again as their kids continue to grow out of their clothes.

Aim High

Knowing this, as well as knowing that you can't compete with discount apparel retailers like Wal-Mart, Sears, and Target—where thousands of sensible parents we don't care about are shopping—you're going to have to develop a more fashion-oriented niche aimed at upper- and middle-income parents. These parents tend to spend more on their own clothing and are willing to pay a premium for their children's clothes. You also won't have to worry about the fact that Sears carries the same outfit for $5 to $10 less.

As an upscale children's retailer, you can target parents who tend to think of their children as extensions of themselves. The way their children are dressed and the degree of stylishness directly reflect their sense of taste. That's what you can cash in on, and in the right market, a children's clothing store can be a strong business.

Aside from offering a higher quality of merchandise, children's boutiques fill a service void. You will not find a cashier at Sears helping customers into the dressing rooms with their clothes or cooing over small children. This fact has contributed to the rise in popularity of finer children's apparel shops in recent years.

The Baby Boom

Cashing in on the baby boomers' baby boomlet of the last decade, the children's apparel market increased by 2 percent over the previous year for a total sales of $27 billion and is considered among the fastest-growing segments of the overall retail market. Well, we've got the Baby Gap to thank for that, as well as the fact that, like their parents, kids today are getting fashion cues from TV, whether it's the WB network or MTV.

Another important consideration will be the inclusion of accessories in your store. "Every apparel retail store now carries kids' clothes, so there's competition everywhere," says Marcia Sauters, who owns My New Friends, a children's store in a Los Angeles suburb. Her unique boutique displays many hand-painted specialty items that she sells in addition to clothes. "This means that part of developing your niche should include branching out into accessories. In my case, we sell personalized gifts like blankets, suitcases, and clothing, many of which I do myself to cut down on costs. We sell a lot of $30 gifts to pay the rent."

And even though Sauter's store happens to be located in a first-class neighborhood, there are no guarantees. As she explains, "Someone in Nebraska might do all right, but Southern California is a tough, competitive market. True, there might be more money in my little neighborhood than in most other states, but that doesn't necessarily mean those people are spending it on their children's clothes. A lot of wealthy people buy their kids' clothes at Target."

Tip...

Smart Tip
Traditionally, children's apparel stores have carried clothing for infants to ten-year-olds. As competition from big apparel and discount chains grows, that has changed, and what you carry will depend largely on your location and your proximity to a mall.

Make Fashion Fun

While an organized look is still high on the list of priorities in a children's and/or teen-oriented store, you'll probably also want to create an element of fun as well. For a children's store, "fun" can be as simple as a colorful window display or as involved as an interior decor that includes pastel-colored walls and a designated play area.

Some ideas that work well in a children's store are the use of pastel colors, which creates a nursery-like atmosphere, colored graphics or cutouts on the wall, and brighter carpet and lighting than what we'd suggest for an adult-oriented apparel store. Some experts even recommend coming up with a theme for your store, which for kids might be a superhero, circus, or cartoon character motif.

Again, if you're worried about cost, you might think about turning over your store interior to students at a local art school.

Sales: Speedy yet Sincere

Face it. It's a pain in the neck to shop for children, and parents with money don't enjoy it any more than parents who are bargain shoppers. As the store owner, you're going to want to modify our T.O. rule into that accounting acronym FIFO, which stands for first in, first out. Your mission as children's apparel store owner will be to outfit that child as quickly, painlessly, and profitably as possible.

Keep in mind that, even with four-year-old twin tornadoes, you'll still want to give your customers sufficient time to browse and come to you with specific questions. At the same time, make them feel at home and admired as parents. Admiring their cute kids is one way of getting in a parent's good graces.

The Terrible Teens: Jeans Are Keen

We can't write a children's clothing chapter without talking about teens. The topic of teens doesn't warrant its own chapter because many women's and men's specialty stores carry clothing that caters to a limitless age group. On top of that, many children's stores—we are not talking baby stores here—now include sizes appropriate for teens.

One of the people who tracks fashion preferences among teenagers is Irma Zandl, president of the New York City-based Zandl Group, a trend-spotting company that does nationwide surveys. She says that, as might be expected, jeans are the single most popular item in teenagers' wardrobes.

Like everything else in fashion, the interest in denim and jeans is cyclical. In the 1950s, movie stars like Marilyn Monroe and James Dean made wearing jeans look glamorous and sexy. In the '60s, jeans became a symbol of social rebellion. In the late '70s, Calvin Klein and Ralph Lauren got into the act and sparked a craze for designer jeans. This trend carried well into the '80s with new designers like Gloria Vanderbilt and Armani jumping into the fray. Black jeans heralded the '90s and eventually gave way to a variety of colors. The new millennium discovered jeans have bling with the addition of crystal beads and rhinestones.

According to the NPD Group, a Port Washington, New York retail research company, dollar sales for women's jeans in 2005 were $7.6 billion, up nearly 10 percent. Women's premium jeans (jeans priced over $100) accounted for 18 percent of denim sales

> **Fun Fact**
> Adult-teen fashions are so interchangeable these days that 40-year-old mothers are often buying their own blouses and accessories at teen-oriented stores because they're cheaper.

The Guy-Factor

If you thought men were fashion-challenged, what about their younger counterparts? These young fellas also have a desire to look cool, but typically rely on TV shows, magazines, rock groups, and school friends to help pull it together. What they don't always understand is just because their favorite boy's band is sporting rhinestone-studded bananas, doesn't mean they should. Teen guys often don't know what's hip and what isn't and you can turn them (and their friends) into loyal customers if you can stop them from making a fashion faux pas.

Stock up with the classics: jeans, khaki pants, T-shirts, sweatshirts, sweaters. And don't forget the accessories like neck chains (boys don't call them "necklaces"), bracelets, watches, hats, and visors. Know what's out (cargo pants) and what's in (hoodies). Of course, anything sports-inspired is definitely hot.

in U.S. department stores, up from 12 percent in 2004. Plus, these young women needed something to wear with their jeans and so, they shelled out over $10 billion on T-shirts, posting a 10 percent spurt in that category last year.

Premium denim wear has exploded on the market, in part thanks to the teenagers who have adopted jeans as a school uniform. And it has become fashion-driven. Today's teens want their jeans cut down to god-knows-where, well-fitted, and ready to rock. But like the fickle female, those criteria can change with amazing speed.

"We're in a fashion cycle, and when you're in a fashion cycle, it can shift so fast," says Bonnie Junell, a Nordstrom vice president and merchandise manager for junior girls. "Fit-and-flare is the new basic. We used to have jeans folded on shelves on the back wall. Now you have to hang them so they see the style."

The Tween Years

Preteens are the awkward years between nine and twelve where fad-loving, trend-following, filled-with-attitude youngsters struggle for independence, while still needing boundaries. It's a tough place to be, but fortunately it's only for a few years.

Preadolescence no longer exists as a gentle segue into the teenage years, because ten is the "new fifteen" and marketers have christened this new social anomaly a "tween."

"There's no question there's a deep trend, not a passing fad, toward kids getting older younger," says research psychologist Michael Cohen, President of Arc

Consulting, a public policy, education, and marketing research firm in New York. "This is not just on the coasts. There are no real differences geographically."

Even before this niche found a name, marketers began to see its power during the late '80s. Jordache Jeans was one of the first manufacturers to take advantage of the evolving trend by appealing directly to adolescents with questionably inappropriate ads. However, the commercials were soon pulled because <gasp> parents watch TV too. Plus, they have deeper pockets which gives them more buying clout.

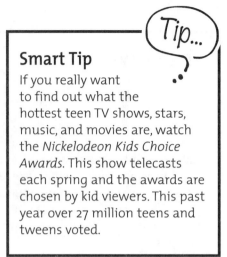

Smart Tip

If you really want to find out what the hottest teen TV shows, stars, music, and movies are, watch the *Nickelodeon Kids Choice Awards.* This show telecasts each spring and the awards are chosen by kid viewers. This past year over 27 million teens and tweens voted.

Fortunately, today's ads for tweens don't go in for the shock value; however, they still try to charm young viewers by appealing to their streak of independence and desire to appear as young sophisticates.

According to many of the apparel entrepreneurs interviewed for this book, today there's often little differentiation between what parents and their kids consider fashionable. You will find a lot of the same clothing and accessories in *Seventeen* as you will in *Vogue*. Part of this is because young people are increasingly influenced by culture and the media, including what they see on television and in magazines, as well as what their friends are wearing.

Stat Fact

According to the National Retail Federation, parents expect to spend an average $527 per child on back-to-school shopping in the fall, with teens expected to contribute more than $29 of their own money on top of that. Ranking highest on the shopping list for both kids and parents is apparel, with parents admitting that the greatest influence on the final purchase comes from the kids.

If you're looking to open a store that caters strictly to tween girls or boys or simply want to add a junior department to your children's store and move merchandise, here's a tip from T.J. Reid, an apparel industry expert, speaker, and author. Include your local teen clientele—and their mothers—in store events, such as fashion shows and promotional activities. (We talk a lot more about general customer involvement in Chapter 13, but since this is teen-specific, we thought we'd give you a heads-up here.)

So, to sum it up for tweens—treat them just like teens. At least when they're in your store.

Teens (and tweens) rule and it's essential to get a handle on male and female teen fashion throes and woes from the onset. As with male and female adult fashions, pay attention to what the kids are wearing at the malls, schools, skat-

Cool Kids' Stuff

If you're looking for some interesting lines to carry in your store that will help you specialize and form a niche, look at:

- ○ *Tot Towels (www.tottowels.com)*. Unique children's hooded towel wraps, cover-ups made of heavy-duty 100 percent cotton towels.
- ○ *Wee Golf (www.weegeneration.com)*. Pint-size golf clothes.
- ○ *T-Shirt Connection (http://t-shirtconnection.com)*. Designer T-shirts with logos such as trucks, tractors, and teddy bears.
- ○ *Peek-a-Boo Kids (www.peekabookids.com)*. High-end, brand-name clothing for boys, girls, and infants.
- ○ *Miracle Baby (www.mymiraclebaby.com)*. Unique, handmade fashions for babies and children, featuring boutique and pageant wear.

ing rinks, and other teen hangouts. Flip through the magazines and TV channels. Watch *Drake and Josh* on Nickelodeon or *That's So Raven* on the Disney Channel. Become cyber-smart and troll the internet highways for the latest and greatest information on teen fashions. There are hundreds of web sites that can put you in the "need to know" place you need to be.

Born-Again Business Opportunity

Statisticians tell us that birth rates are historically cyclical. With more and more futurists predicting that we are on the verge of another baby boom or at least a boomlet, the children's apparel industry is gearing up for a new period of growth.

The prechoolers you may cater to today will be the tweens and teens of tomorrow. And, of course, the cycle will definitely shift again, so wherever you decide to start will be a good place to begin.

Exclusively Yours
Specialty
Boutiques

There is a re-emerging face in retail and it's called the "specialty shop." These unique stores and quaint little shops have been resurging all over the country on the heels of the latest advancement made in the ultimate shopping experience: "lifestyle centers," which are picking up where shopping malls have left off.

Like the mall, these Main Street style centers have retail chains, movie theatres, and restaurants; however, specialty shops are much larger in numbers. This is because the centers aren't reliant on department stores and big chain names to keep them afloat. But mall lovers shouldn't despair because malls still outnumber lifestyle centers 10–1, and they aren't going anywhere.

Specialty shops are gaining in popularity everywhere—not just lifestyle centers—because they offer consumers uncommon, exceptional products that are usually not found in chain or department stores. They are essentially the antidote to mass manufacturing. The following are samples of different specialty shops that have had a big impact on today's retail clothing market.

Boutique Is Chic

What's chic about a boutique? A boutique is a small specialty shop that offers unusual and distinctive merchandise that wouldn't ordinarily be found in a traditional clothing or department store. In addition to the unique apparel, accessories, and gifts, patrons are also charmed by the quality customer service and reasonable prices these quaint little shops offer.

Boutique merchandise can range from everyday, contemporary apparel to one-of-a-kind haute couture worn by fashionable celebrities. The Secret Garden, a Victorian-style boutique owned by Richard and Bobigene Fent in Branson, Missouri, features stylish, well-designed day and evening wear along with beautiful jewelry, gifts, and accessories. "When visitors enter our boutique they often feel as if they have stepped into a bygone era," says Bobigene.

Because a number of their private labeled garments are not reproduced, their shop is frequented by some of the area's top female entertainers such as Alison Krause and Lorrie Morgan. In addition to their vintage-inspired clothing, The Secret Garden also carries other trendy brands such as Spencer Alexis, Sweet Romance, and Biscotti, as well as high-end clothing and gifts for children and infants.

So where do you find all of this great stuff? Start locally. Some of the best products are right under your nose. The Fents' best sellers are handmade, one-of-a-kind garments made by a private tailor. Marcia Sauters, who owns the children's boutique in Santa Monica, California, has several local people who provide high-quality merchandise like hand-knit infant sweaters or personalized gift items. Be

Fun Fact

Many of today's big players started out as small neighborhood boutique owners like Nordstrom, Inc., whose humble beginnings came about in 1901 selling shoes in Seattle, Washington.

sure to read Chapter 11, Getting the Goods, to find other sources for locating merchandise.

You may have also noticed that boutiques have more flexibility with location choices. In addition to the recommendations made in Chapter 8, boutiques can set up shop almost anywhere. Both the Fents and Marcia Sauters operate out of picturesque little bungalows in strategically located parts of their cities. But if you need to start out on a smaller scale, other alternatives could be a mall kiosk, a corner of a salon, or a space within a large department store. In rural areas it is not unusual to find a residence that has one or two rooms used for a home boutique.

Vintage: Old World Couture

If you love to shop 'til you drop by spending hours looking for timeless fashions from different periods, then the start of a bonafide vintage clothing store could be your own rags to riches story. Celebrities, performers, collectors, designers, and regular folks frequent vintage clothing shops for different reasons. But the biggest is because of the unique, outdated styles that can't be found anywhere else. Many clothes hounds like to stand out in the crowd and owning an unusual, one-of-a-kind ensemble gives these glamour pusses a distinctive edge.

What Is Vintage Clothing?

Vintage wear is clothing and accessories that are no longer made, hard to find, and in big demand. These fashions come from another era such as the 18th, 19th, or 20th century or basically anything made more than 25 years ago. Often when people think about vintage, what usually comes to mind are styles worn in movies like *Ziegfeld Follies* (1946), *Designing Woman* (1957), or *Saturday Night Fever* (1977). Even more recent styles like the designs worn in *Footloose* (1984) and *Pretty in Pink* (1986) might now be considered "vintage." However, you should note that polyester is still way uncool.

Fans of vintage wear love poodle skirts, flapper dresses, crinolines, and cat eye glasses. Victorian and western wear are also hot items, especially for folks in show-biz. However, women's vintage wear is not the only desirable

Fun Fact
Many celebrities favor vintage fashions, like Reese Witherspoon who bought a '50s Dior dress in Paris that she wore to the 78th Academy Awards. Or Kiera Knightly who strolled down the same red carpet beautifully adorned in vintage Bulgari jewelry from the 1930s. Even leading men have been known to select timeless formalwear, such as Jeremy Irons who wore a vintage Giorgio Armani tux to the Oscars one year.

category. Menswear such as Hawaiian shirts, zoot suits, spectator shoes, hats, canes, and handpainted neckties are also in big demand.

Where Can You Find Vintage Wear?

Vintage wear can be found just about anywhere that secondhand clothing is sold including vintage shops, consignment shops, thrift stores, and estate sales. Even garage and yard sales can sometimes be fruitful.

VINTAGE SHOPS

Naturally these shops have the best selections, but they will also have the highest prices. Catering to their clientele, clothing will often be grouped by era or decade with a knowledgeable staff ready to assist with any questions. So start asking—even if you don't plan on buying.

CONSIGNMENT SHOPS AND THRIFT STORES

This can be a hit or miss process; however, you will find lower prices—especially at thrift stores. Smaller charity- or church-run secondhand shops often have more vintage items than a large Salvation Army-type thrift store. You will be on your own if you have any questions, so do your homework beforehand. Check the items carefully for any flaws, because most of these stores have a no return policy. To find local thrift shops in your area, go to: www.thethriftshopper.com.

ESTATE SALES

Estate sales are one of the best ways to find vintage items and heirlooms. These are generally held when someone has passed away or is relocating to a smaller facility and needs to liquidate and dispose of their belongings. Look for estate sales in the classified section of your local newspaper. You can also contact local auction houses in your area to see when they will host their next estate sale.

GARAGE, YARD, AND RUMMAGE SALES

You will find the best bargains at these types of sales; however, they entail a lot of running around. Look for garage sales in older, affluent areas as they often have high-end, designer clothing and accessories. Community-wide garage sales are a huge bonus, and don't pass by unadvertised garage sales along the way.

ONLINE AUCTIONS

The internet is a great way to find vintage clothing and accessories. There are hundreds of online vintage stores featuring bargains and hard-to-find items; not to mention auction sites such as eBay for which vintage wear is a staple. This can be a timesaver for you because these sellers have already scoured the estate and garage

---

Know Your Stuff

Vintage haute couture is always a top seller, as are unique, custom-made styles and designer labels from other eras. But just because a garment is older than dirt doesn't necessarily mean that it is deemed worthy—especially if it has dirt or any other defects on it. The quality of the apparel, along with the style and design, is what will place it in the collector's closet. Tips for spotting authentic vintage wear are:

- ○ Plastic zippers did not originate until after the 1960s
- ○ Men's suit coats from the 1940s had a handy-dandy button hole in the lapel that also served as a flower holder
- ○ Women's dresses and slacks had side zippers
- ○ Fabric care instructions were not sewn into garments until after the '60s
- ○ Vintage Hawaiian shirts are 100 percent rayon with wood or coconut shell buttons
- ○ Most clothing was made to order up until the mid-1950s, so don't bypass unfamiliar labels
- ○ Buttons made of jet, brass, bone, pearl, and the button holes themselves are characteristics of quality craftsmanship.

To familiarize yourself with vintage designs, study old magazines and patterns to see how they are constructed. Teach yourself how to recognize true vintage wear by analyzing its style, fabric, label, and the way it's sewn. Research online auctions featuring period clothing and join focus groups to network with industry professionals. Purchase vintage clothing pricing guides so that you can educate yourself on their values. This will especially come in handy if you are getting ready to pass over a $20 dingy leather jacket that was made by the East West Musical Instruments Co. in the 1960s and is now worth over $3,000.

---

sales, identifying hot-selling items and spotting potential flaws. You can also reverse the trend by becoming an online vintage reseller yourself.

FAMILY AND FRIENDS

Get the word out that you are on the prowl for vintage clothing. There is probably a treasure trove in Uncle Bernie's or Grandma Gertie's closet. Of course they may think you are a bit daft for wanting to pay them for these "old things," but it'll give them something to talk about on Bingo night.

ADVERTISE

Put up notices in senior citizen centers or take out ad space in publications that reach audiences who may have vintage apparel.

Secondhand Style: Selling on Consignment

Although the lines are a little blurry, there is a distinct difference between a used clothing store and a vintage shop. Secondhand clothing is gently used apparel that may be outdated by a couple of seasons, but still has a lot of good wear left. People typically buy secondhand clothing for practical, economical reasons, while vintage fashions are more often purchased to satisfy an emotional response.

Owning a consignment shop is less risky than a traditional retail clothing store because you don't have to pay for your inventory until it sells. Kind of like free inventory. And if it doesn't sell, you are off the hook; the items are either given the big heave-ho to the consignor or donated to charity. As with vintage wear, consignment clothing shops often specialize in specific fashions like bridal, children, maternity, special occasion, plus size or vintage.

Although most consignment clothing stores feature secondhand styles, that's not always the case. Marcia Sauters, who owns My New Friends in Santa Monica, California, has a consignment arrangement for some beautifully hand-knit infant sweaters. "These are a little more high-end than I would normally carry," she says. "I wouldn't want to buy them outright, so I sell them on consignment."

Stocking Up

If you are initially stocking your store with your own inventory, secondhand clothing can be found at the same places discussed for locating vintage wear or bought in bulk from commercial non-profit thrift stores. If you choose the latter, expect to

Tip...

Smart Tip

Check store inventory for expired items at least every two weeks. Handle these slow movers in accordance with your policy and get them out of the shop. Frequent customers will recognize and remember unsold apparel, which doesn't make for a lasting impression.

receive large boxes of clothing sight unseen that you will have to weed through and sort into piles of "fabulous," "possibility" and "eew, gross."

But as you get up and running, most of the secondhand fashions you sell will come in the form of "consignments." What this essentially means is that people will bring you clothing to be resold in your shop and you will keep a predetermined percentage of the sale.

Items that are in good condition—preferably "like new"—can bring top dollar. Before accepting them, be sure to check garments for tears, stains, or other blemishes. If something has a ripped seam or missing button and is otherwise in good shape, patch it up to be resold for a higher profit.

Operating Procedures

Running a consignment shop introduces a whole new set of policies and procedures besides those of a traditional retail clothing store. For instance, you'll need to decide:

- What types of inventory items are acceptable—designer labels only, vintage wear, infant and children's clothing, seasonal, shoes and accessories, etc.?
- Will the consignment period be 120, 90, or 60 days?
- Will expired items be returned to the consignor or donated to charity?
- What the consignor split will be: 50/50, 60/40?
- Will you accept "walk-ins" or should consignors make an appointment before coming into the shop?
- Who is responsible for lost or damaged items while in the shop owner's possession?
- What are the insurance implications?

Keep track of your inventory and accounts by using intake sheets—aka contracts. These are one to two page forms that list your policies, store hours, and contact information for both parties, in addition to a description of the item(s) to be sold. Most importantly, the consignor must sign the intake sheet acknowledging their

Tip...

Smart Tip

Web Access Consignment International (WACI) software has been specially designed to start and manage a consignment business by tracking inventory, managing customers' accounts, printing checks and monthly statements, creating inventory and financial reports. It can be downloaded online at: http://www.los-gatos.ca.us/los_gatos/businesses/the_web works/waci.

understanding and acceptance of the shop's terms. Be sure to provide the consignor with a copy of the intake sheet which will also suffice as a receipt.

Here Comes the Bride

It actually surprises some people when they discover bridal shops are not run by sweet, doddering, little old ladies. Oh no, these are businesses (as in BIG) operated by contemporary, knowledgeable entrepreneurs who know what it takes to plan a successful wedding. More than $10 billion a year is spent on weddings and receptions, with wedding gowns and bridesmaids' dresses taking a $1.2 billion chunk of that market.

For many entrepreneurs, opening a bridal shop is a dream come true. But it doesn't take long to realize this is not a fairy tale, and you really need to love the business. First and foremost, you should be a people person who is willing to listen to customers so you can understand their wishes. Brides are by nature a difficult lot to deal with. (The same can also be said for moms, bridesmaids, and even grooms.) The first-time bride doesn't understand the process of selecting and purchasing a wedding gown and how different it is from buying other attire. And we're not even taking into account some of the Bridezellas you will encounter, who are in a class all by themselves. Scary!

In a 2005 survey conducted by Leflein Associates, Inc., brides said that finding the perfect wedding dress was the second most stressful part of planning a wedding. (Finding and securing a location was the first.) Why are brides so anxious? The exorbitant cost of the dream gown topped the list at 55 percent, closely followed by the inability to try on different gowns in their size (45 percent), and limited selections (32 percent). Finally, 30 percent said the lack of one-stop bridal shopping rounded out their frustration when trying on wedding gowns. This is where you come in.

You may decide to carry wedding gowns exclusively or include bridal accessories such as veils, headpieces, shoes, gloves, and jewelry. Adding bridesmaids' and other special occasion dresses to your inventory will also help to increase the store's coffers.

A popular alternative for the independent bridal store owner is to become a full-service bridal shop. You can offer lots of fun extras such as invitations, party favors, shower gifts, lingerie, alterations, and tuxedo rentals. Many

Stat Fact

In a recent study done by the Fairfield Bridal Group, the average cost for a traditional American wedding is fast approaching $30,000. This figure represents a 73 percent increase over the past 15 years. "The bridal industry is now a life stage that encompasses fashion, travel, home furnishings, and more," says Daniel Lagani, vice president and publisher of the Fairchild Bridal Group.

bridal shops also offer wedding consulting and planning as part of their services, which can generate additional revenue. At the very least, it would be very beneficial to develop relationships with local vendors so that you can recommend wedding planners, photographers, florists, and reception venues in the area. Naturally, they would extend the same courtesy to you, so networking is a must and a plus.

Even more than becoming wildly prosperous, you want to be known as a "reputable" bridal shop. Although bridal stores are plentiful in some areas—decent, reliable ones are not. How do you achieve this exalted status? Via the brides themselves. These girls talk—a lot—and they share information about what shops have the best customer service and which ones will take them for a ride.

Setting Up Shop

To get up and running, bridal shops initially invest several thousands of dollars in sample inventory. Gowns typically retail from $200 to $3000, with an average gown selling for $800. As an owner, you will work as a "middleman" with several designers and manufacturers from whom you will order a variety of different sample styles—usually in sizes 10 and 12. From your (hopefully) wide selection, the bride will come in and

---

Diva Designers

Not all designers and manufacturers are created equal and there are some things that novice bridal retailers need to be aware of: such as the dreaded "minimums," where certain designers insist shops purchase a specific amount of their sample gowns twice a year. And if, heaven forbid, a store owner misses a season, the designer will drop them like a cellular phone call in a dead zone. Some mischievous designers try to send stores "mystery" samples that the store owner did not order or want, but is expected to stock and pay for. You should also know that most designers hate returns, even when the problem originated on their end such as the wrong size or damaged goods.

On the other hand, you will find that some bridal manufacturers can be quite helpful by assisting you with planning your inventory. Some will even provide online educational courses regarding bridal consulting, inventory control, and other topics.

The moral of this story is to develop a thick skin and be prepared to stand your ground. If a designer is simply too difficult to deal with, cross them off the list and move on. As mentioned previously, there are tons of designers to choose from.

choose her dream gown. You will then take accurate measurements to be provided to the manufacturer, secure a delivery date, and collect a deposit. If you do not have your own alterations person, be sure to provide the bride with the name(s) of a local seamstress who can do this task, if necessary—and it almost always is.

Although there are more than 200 bridal gown designers, your shop will probably only carry 10 to 12 lines. So, what happens if the bride wants to order a gown from a designer with whom you are not affiliated? If your networking skills are up to speed you can still make the sale by calling another shop (preferably not in the same town) and asking them to order it for you. Of course, your profit margin will not be as high because the other shop will also take a percentage. This process is called "trans-shipping" and you really need to be on your toes when using it. Make sure this is a reliable bridal shop that will not leave you holding the bag. If they say the dress will be delivered in four months, give yourself a cushion by telling your bride it will be six. If any problems occur during this process it will be up to the other shop owner to talk to the manufacturer, not you. In other words you have no control, although you're the one the unhappy bride will be ranting at.

Owning a bridal shop requires additional policies and procedures besides those of a traditional retail clothing store. For example:

- *Deposits.* As part of your policies you will need to decide on the amount of a deposit required and when the balance has to be paid in full. The industry standard is 50 percent which is due when the customer places her order. The balance is due when the dress is picked up or before it is shipped to the recipient. No garment should be altered unless it has been paid in full.

- *Refunds.* You will need to determine when and if a deposit is refundable. In most cases it is not. Each wedding gown or bridesmaid's dress is different in style, size, and color and chances are slim to none that another individual is going to pick that same exact dress. This is the biggest reason why manufacturers will usually not accept returns.

- *Dates of delivery.* Despite promised delivery dates, savvy bridal shop owners know which manufacturers run chronically late and will pad the time by a few weeks. You may want to do this with all of your designers until your insight has fully developed in this regard. This will help to delay frantic calls of "Is my dress there yet?" or "Don't make me call Daddy."

- *Put it in writing.* It's hard to remember what you told a prospective customer last week or last month, let alone last year. If you offer free alterations, a 10 percent discount, or anything else that is not standard, write it down. Include the bride's contact information, wedding date, favorite wedding gown designers, etc. Keep track on a computer, in a three-ring binder or card index file and use the information to contact the bride when you receive new inventory or have a sale so you can remain on her radar.

- *Privacy issues.* Protect your customers' privacy by safeguarding their personal information. Some bridal shop owners have bad manners and sell information to wedding vendors and merchants, who in turn inundate the poor bride with phone calls and junk mail from Boutonnieres by Bunny and Tom's Tunnel of Love Drive-Thru Chapel.

- *Perks.* Many bridal shops offer special incentives to their customers. For example, throw in a free steaming when a wedding gown is purchased from you. Other services could include free delivery or a discount on cleaning and preservation.

> **Beware!**
> Sometimes unscrupulous bridal shop owners remove the manufacturers' tags from wedding dresses making it impossible to know if the gown is a designer label or a knock-off. The Federal Textile Products Identification Act, Title 15, Sec 70, prohibits this type of activity. Violators can be fined up to $5,000 and peek through the bars of a jail cell for a year.

- *By appointment only.* Although most bridal shops have regular store hours, it's not uncommon for them to schedule appointments for fittings, especially if the bride needs to come after hours or she has a large wedding party who all want to come at the same time. This ensures that you will have enough staff members available and everyone is taken care of.

- *All sales are final.* Seriously, no cancellations should be allowed. Make sure the customer signs a receipt that clearly states this policy loud and clear. Otherwise, a naughty bride could decide to swing by after the wedding to drop off the dress for some honeymoon cash. The only exceptions to this rule are extreme circumstances for which you will have to rely upon your finely honed powers of discrimination. Even then you should only offer a store credit—not a cash refund.

Closed Inventory—or Not

Some bridal shops have "closed inventory" that prevents browsers from pawing through the racks. These salon-type stores are reminiscent of a bygone era when salespeople in ritzy stores would bring out gowns one at a time to show customers. This type of preferential treatment is nice when it is carried out in style. The key to success is understanding exactly what the bride is looking for. Closed inventory can create frustration when the bride is at the beginning stage of her wedding gown search and doesn't really know what she wants, or the salesperson is not a good visionary and doesn't have a clue what to look for. Yes, your samples will stay fresher longer if you and your staff are the only ones handling them, but the inconvenience to potential customers who just want to browse may outweigh other drawbacks. Besides, you can always sell the sample dresses at a big discount and replace them with new ones.

Made to Order:
Private Label Branding

Private label clothing are garments with a label that can be exclusive to a department store or a small, specialty boutique. They can be designed in-house or by outside manufacturers (often out of the country). These labels are an important weapon for clothing retailers, and they are on the rise. Many specialty clothing store and boutique owners like Bobigene and Richard Fent of Branson, Missouri, know the value of having a brand they can call their own. "Some of our shop's clothing items are handmade, one-of-a-kind pieces, featuring The Secret Garden's own private label," says Bobigene. "Our best sellers are the vintage-inspired apparel that is custom made by a private tailor specifically for our boutique."

Make It Personal

Personal shoppers are a benefit that many stores and boutiques offer to enhance a customer's experience while increasing sales. They perform a variety of functions including advising the customer what apparel is in fashion, what styles and colors look best on an individual, selecting an outfit based on the customer's tastes, and even help plan an entire wardrobe. Some personal shoppers are multi-talented and can hold small in-store seminars on color analysis or accessorizing with flair.

Sometimes a customer simply doesn't have the time to shop or just needs to find a quick gift. Whatever the reason, not only does the customer benefit from this service but so does the shop owner. The personal shopper selects items from the store's collection and then makes arrangements to hand deliver or ship the merchandise. Many people love this one-on-one attention (seriously, who wouldn't) and quickly turn into loyal, repeat customers.

Some personal shoppers are staff members employed by the shop itself, while others are freelancers and work only when needed. If you offer personal shopping to your customers, you will need to decide whether this is a free service or if you should charge a small fee.

Of course you don't need to have your own tailor to use private label branding. There are hundreds of manufacturers who will make the clothing and apply the labels for you; or you can send them the clothing and labels to have them professionally reapplied. No one will ever know. You can hook up with some of these folks through the Private Label Manufacturer's Association (www.plma.com).

The question that begs to be asked is why would a shop owner want to promote their own brand next to a nationally recognized designer label? Often there are cost advantages for the consumer, plus retailers have more control over product development and marketing when they use private labels.

Fun Fact

Many commercial retailers have been using private branding for years such as K-Mart's Martha Stewart label and Dillard's line of menswear designed by Daniel Cremieux. And although Saks Fifth Avenue discontinued its private labels a couple of years ago, they are a hallmark for Nordstrom, whose five top brands make up 20 percent of their annual sales.

It takes a while to establish your own brand, so it's doubtful that your private label will be an overnight success. That's because there is so much chaos in the marketing environment that it's hard to be seen or heard right away. But don't be discouraged—consistency and time will pay off—especially if you have a premium private label.

6

Style and Substance
Laying Your Foundation

In this chapter we'll talk seriously about what kind of fashion statement you want to make, from choosing your apparel store's name to determining how to legally operate your business.

A Name to Remember

If you are not taking over a family or other person's apparel store and are instead hanging your own brand-new shingle, lucky you—at least where creativity is concerned. You might have to play catch-up on certain business matters, but you also get to come up with your own name.

Depending on what your marketing research has revealed to you about the clientele in your store's location, you'll either be able to let your imagination run wild (New York, Los Angeles, or San Francisco) or you might want to err on the side of caution or good taste (Palm Beach, Florida, or Grosse Pointe, Michigan).

From an advertising standpoint—which we'll go into greater depth in Chapter 13—and for obvious reasons, the easiest but maybe not the most exciting name for your business is one that describes your apparel store, like Main Street Clothing for Women, or Plus Size Fashions, or Mike's Menswear. Yes, it's a yawn.

If you're opening your business in a small town where your father is the longtime mayor or your family's name carries as much weight as Kennedy does in Hyannisport, simply using your last name may carry enough cachet to get the foot traffic flowing. If your store is in the same small town where you had a reputation for egging neighbors' houses or having wild parties as a kid, you might want to use someone else's last name.

If you use your full name in the title of the business, such as "Jonathan Harrington Clothing Co.," you will (if you pay your bills on time) improve your personal credit as you build your store's credit—and you'll build prestige in the community at the same time. It won't take long for people to recognize your name and associate it with your business.

Let's go to the worst-case scenario and say that your last name is something that doesn't easily roll off the tongue, like Stephanopolous or Humperdink, or you're simply looking for any excuse to use your creative naming skills. That's fine, as long as you make your brainstorming relative.

Here's what we mean by relativity. In 1976, when one apparel entrepreneur opened, he wanted to come up with a name that would have some longevity in associating him with the upscale value of the clothing in his store. He came up with The Wooden Nickel for reasons he says are best spelled out on his store's promo piece: "Historically, the term wooden nickel

> **Beware!**
> When stores strive for nothing more than uniqueness by using nondescriptive names, many potential customers may pass them by, not realizing what's inside. This also applies to arty or off-the-wall signs that don't provide clues to the clothes you sell.

described a token that was used as a medium of exchange. It had a value when redeemed at the business that issued them. Today, The Wooden Nickel is still a symbol of value. It's classic. It's contemporary. It's menswear. It's womens wear. It's you."

Here's what we mean by nonrelativity. Another apparel store owner says that since day one she's regretted naming her store The Classy Oak. "When I first bought the store there was lots of wood in it and the landlord built an oak counter that sort of served as a centerpiece for the store," says the owner, who can laugh about it now after all these years. "But I have to tell you that today people still walk in looking for end tables because they think we're a furniture store. Your name is important, so think about it carefully."

Smart Tip

The cost of filing a fictitious name notice ranges from $10 to $100. Call your bank and ask if it requires a fictitious name registry or certificate to open a business account. If so, find out how to get one.

Doing Business As . . .

After you come up with a name for your apparel store, you'll have to register it as a dba, or doing business as, in your local newspaper.

Essentially, registering your store's name means that you need to check whether someone else has already come up with your name and then, assuming no one has, pay a fee to register it as your own. If the name is already in use, you'll need to choose something different.

This process varies from state to state. In Florida, for example, you call the office of the secretary of state, whose office sends you a registration form. You mail back the completed form, the registration fee, and a form from your local newspaper verifying that you've registered your fictitious name or dba for one week. Generally, the newspaper that prints the legal notice for your business name will file the necessary papers with the county for a small fee.

Beware!

Until your store has operated successfully as a corporation for many years, you will most likely still have to accept personal liability for any corporate loans made by banks or other financial institutions.

In California, you call your city or county clerk's office, check the roster of business names and complete the registration procedure at the clerk's window. Fictitious-name filings do not apply to corporations in most states unless the corporation is doing business under a name other than its own. We mention this because many apparel store owners, including you, may decide to incorporate due to benefits we'll discuss later. Documents of incorporation have the same effect for businesses as fictitious-name filings have for sole proprietorships and partnerships.

Another reason you'll need a dba? Most banks require you to have one to open an account.

Your Stylish Structure

Apparel store structures will vary. If you start out opening a small store on your own, with no partners, you will be operating as a sole proprietorship.

A sole proprietorship is the easiest method of starting a business. No legal papers are required except a business license and a dba, and no separate income tax returns are necessary.

However, a sole proprietorship has one important disadvantage: Creditors of your business can go after you personally and attach your personal property and bank account.

> **Tip...**
>
> ### Smart Tip
> You can buy partnership agreement forms at just about any stationery store, or you can purchase books like *Form a Partnership: The Complete Legal Guide*, available from Nolo Books. Order online at www.nolo.com or call (800) 728-3555.

A Dynamic Duo

Choosing a partner wisely will be one of the most important things you do when you open your store. To avoid problems:

- ○ Decide beforehand how store duties, like buying, working nights, etc., will be split up, and put them in writing to prevent any misunderstandings.
- ○ Have an out. Talk about a buy-sell agreement early on in case one of you decides to sell out at some point.
- ○ Buy life insurance. If you or your partner dies, a "key man" insurance policy will insure that the surviving store partner will be able to buy out the deceased partner; consult an expert, like an attorney, accountant, or other business expert.

Pondering a Partnership?

A partnership of two or more people is more dangerous than a sole proprietorship because each partner is responsible for the other's actions. In any legal or

Beware!
Never form a partnership on only a handshake and verbal agreement; always have a formal contract drawn up by a lawyer.

creditor action, each of you will be sued personally, with your property and your bank accounts attached. If one partner skips town, any others are, well, out of luck. Also, when people contribute assets, such as cash, to a partnership, all they get for their generosity is an equity in store assets. Hint: The more generous you are, the more you have to lose if your store fails.

The most realistic way to start an apparel business is under a corporate structure, because the corporation exists as a separate entity from you and is alone legally responsible for its actions and debts. In other words, you are personally protected in most situations, since you will be an employee of the corporation only, even though you may own all or most of the stock.

The majority of the apparel entrepreneurs we interviewed agreed that this structure makes the most sense, since it protects you from everyone, including your vendors.

Getting Permission

Whenever you open any kind of business, including a clothing store, the bureaucrats get you coming and going with license, permit, and other fees. As an apparel store owner, you'll have to get the following:

- *Business license.* This is just another piece of necessary paperwork that you'll need to open your store—and that you'll want prominently displayed somewhere near your front counter and cash register. Business licenses aren't normally that difficult to get unless you have to go through all that zoning stuff.

- *Sellers permit.* In many states, apparel wholesalers or manufacturers won't sell to you at wholesale prices unless you can show them your sales tax permit or number, also called a sellers permit. With your business license, you can usually get a permit from the State Equalization Board, the State Sales Tax Commission, or the Franchise Tax Board. The important thing about a resale permit is that it allows you to avoid paying sales tax at the time you purchase merchandise from suppliers. The sales tax is then added to the clothing's retail price.

- *Fire department permit.* The fire department requires you to have a permit if you use any flammable material—though we cannot imagine what that would be in an apparel store—or if your store will be occupied by more than several thousand people. You should be so lucky, right?

- *Sign permit.* In some cases, cities have their own ordinances that restrict the size, location, lighting, and type of sign used. Landlords, usually those in malls, may also impose their own restrictions; just make sure you find out what's allowed before you start getting any artistic notions.

- *County permits.* The ladder of bureaucracy is endless, and you'll find that if you open your store just outside city limits, you will have to collect yet another permit.

- *Federal licenses.* If you're conducting business across state lines, or if your store is running ads in another state, you have to contact the Federal Trade Commission about a federal license.

A Nonhostile Takeover

Taking over an existing apparel store may seem like a simple, or at least the most logical, shortcut for new store owners. If you're not lucky enough to have inherited a business, don't worry. You can find ads for stores for sale in apparel industry trade publications, or by searching online at sites like Business Nation (www.businessnation.com). This book's Appendix will also list additional sources.

Provided the previous store owner was on the up and up about his financial records, and the store isn't suddenly the only building standing on an otherwise demolished block in a ghost town, there are many advantages to taking over someone's successful store. You have an established income from the start, a ready-made clientele, established records of sales and purchases, a viable customer mailing list, established manufacturer and vendor resources and clothing lines, an existing stock of inventory, established goodwill within your community, and a proven location.

But there are also disadvantages to buying a pre-owned store—namely, if you're dealing with an owner who is not honest with you about all the things we mentioned above. Let's say the owner had a partner from whom he skimmed profits, or he cheated his vendors, or she didn't pay taxes for the last five years, or the building is rotting. Even one of these things could leave your store doomed. Think SS—Smart Sleuthing. Whatever you call it, make room for another list and take notes on following:

Bright Idea
Be sure you look into any restrictive ordinances that might, for example, limit the hours of the day when trucks are permitted to load and unload merchandise at your store.

Pass or Play?

Never—we repeat, never—buy a pre-owned store without asking yourself these questions first:

1. Why is the store for sale? Does the owner want to retire, or is the business going downhill?
2. What do the records show in terms of sales volume, growth patterns, and the efficiency of the management?
3. What is the condition of the inventory? Is it fresh and current? Or do you see Izod shirts stacked in the storeroom?
4. What is the store's local image, the status of its goodwill and reputation? If it's good, fine. If it's questionable, it then becomes your problem.
5. What has been the trend of the store's sales over the past five years—up or down or at a standstill?
6. How much of the business will you lose? You won't automatically inherit all the former business, especially if the previous store owner is moving down the block.
7. Is the store worth the asking price?
8. What is the breakdown in sales by departments or categories? If it's a family store, for example, what portion of sales are in men's footwear, or in women's accessories, and so on? This is very important for you to know because it indicates the kind of clientele you'll be working with.
9. What is the quality of the store's brands or lines? Can you retain them with the store's suppliers?
10. What is the store's credit standing—with its resources, with banks, and so on? You'll be inheriting some of the effects of the previous credit rating.
11. What are the store's leasing arrangements with the landlord?
12. Finally, is there room for the store to grow under your new management?

- *Find out why the store is for sale.* This is pretty self-explanatory. If it's not located in a ghost town and not completely enclosed by shopping malls, then ask around.
- *Examine the store's financial records for the past three years and for the year to date.* This is a biggie you might want to get your accountant involved in (more on the value of accountants later).

- *Sit in the store for a few days, observing daily business volume and clientele.* The owner shouldn't have a problem with this, and if he or she does, that's a major red flag.

- *Determine the costs of remodeling and redecorating if the store's decor is to be changed.* If it looks a bit like Armageddon, well, you might want to think twice about buying the place. If it has to be completely gutted but is in a great location, go for it.

- *Determine what existing inventory will suit your plans and should be included in the purchase.* Most sellers deplete their inventory to lower the store's price; even so, any leftover Members Only jackets are a waste of money.

> **Bright Idea**
> Apparel stores are frequently purchased "lock and stock," which means you buy the whole shebang: store fixtures and equipment, inventory, and office and store supplies. You may, however, just opt to buy the fixtures and equipment, leaving yourself free to make your own interior fashion statement.

Franchising Basics

Franchising can be a great way to start a new business because even though you are in business for yourself, you're not alone. You can start your new venture with a proven working model, an enthusiastic team of go-getters, and comprehensive hands-on training.

Here is how it works: The franchisor lends his trademark or trade name and a business model to the franchisee, who pays a royalty and often an initial fee for the right to do business under the franchisor's name and system. The contract binding the two parties is the franchise, but that term is also used to describe the business the franchisee operates.

The best part is the franchisor has already worked the kinks out of the system and is available to help franchisees when new challenges arise. According to the Small Business Administration, most businesses fail from lack of management skills. This is less likely to happen with a franchised business, because your franchisor is there to guide you through the maze of business ownership.

Typically you think of fast food and restaurants when you think of franchising, but virtually every business form has the potential to be franchised, including clothing retailers. In fact, once your business is established, you may want to consider growing it by franchising your concept.

While there are many benefits to owning a franchise (security, training, and marketing power), there are some drawbacks. Perhaps the most significant is the cost of a franchise. The initial franchise fee can run anywhere from a few thousand to several hundred thousand dollars. Then you have continuing royalty payments to the franchisor which are based on the weekly or monthly gross income of your business. Additional expenses may include promotional and advertising fees, operating licenses and permits, insurance, and other costs of running a business.

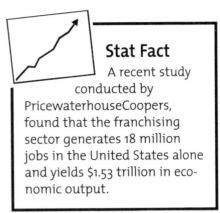

Stat Fact
A recent study conducted by PricewaterhouseCoopers, found that the franchising sector generates 18 million jobs in the United States alone and yields $1.53 trillion in economic output.

Another big drawback is that you have to give up some of your independence. Each franchise is different with how firm its conditions and requirements are; however, you will be bound by the contract to follow and implement the rules and procedures established by the franchisor. For example, if you neglect to pay your royalty fees or misbehave by not meeting performance standards, your franchise could be terminated and you may lose your investment. So, if you like to make your own decisions and "do your own thing," a franchise may not be right for you.

Doing your homework before buying a franchise is essential. You'll be making a large financial commitment and you need to be sure the business will work for you. Much of the information you'll need about a franchise will be provided in the form of a document known as the UFOC, or Uniform Franchise Offering Circular. Under Federal Trade Commission (FTC) rules, you must receive this document at least 10 business days before you are asked to sign any contract or pay any money to the franchisor.

Consultants Are Mentors, Too

We're serious when we say that forming a partnership on a handshake and verbal agreement without a formal contract is unwise. Ditto for a huge bank loan that ends up flushed down the toilet when your partner skips town. That's why many apparel store owners believe that hiring a consultant and/or attorney is the wisest decision they ever made.

Since business consultants are not licensed like doctors and lawyers, you should always ask for some sort of proof of a consultant's expertise, such as their education, professional experience, and, preferably, a list of other apparel-specific clients they've consulted with in the past. Again, this is just a common-sense precaution that shouldn't rankle a potential professional advisor. If it does, then you can figure this person isn't being straight with you and probably has something to hide.

If you don't have time to read magazines or watch television and can afford it, you might want to enlist the services of an apparel consultant like D.L.S.' Fred Derring. As he explains, "We focus on the future and ideas for new ways of marketing, merchandising, advertising, and promoting apparel stores. We then pass those ideas on to our clients and encourage them to keep moving forward and change the way they do business if what they're already doing isn't working."

Consultants, in general, act as purchasing liaisons with manufacturers and vendors. For example: Many small apparel store owners may not have the benefit of knowing all the vendors in New York, the apparel capital of the world. One of a consultant's primary goals is to build

Smart Tip

You can learn more about Debbie Allen's expertise and receive her free six week e-course "Business Success Secrets Revealed" ($100 Value) for free when you sign up online at www.Salesand MarketingSuccess.com.

on relationships with vendors so their smaller specialty store clients can get the same price and to work out invoice payment plans.

On the other coast—almost—Debbie Allen, is now a full-time professional speaker and business consultant specializing in the retailing industry, sharing her knowledge of the industry that she learned from building and selling successful retail stores. She has presented to retailers all over the United States and nine other countries around the world, and is also the author of five books on sales, marketing, and personal growth including *Confessions of Shameless Self Promoters* (McGraw-Hill, 2005) and *Skyrocketing Sales* (Kaplan Business, 2005).

One of the major incentives for Debbie Allen to motivate others was a store owner support group that she attended for years. "These people acted as my consultants and mentors," she recalls. "We would get together and share ideas. I learned many of my buying techniques this way." Sharing and receiving information and support from your peers is priceless, so look to see what types of support and networking groups are available in your area.

A qualified consultant need not hang a shingle outside his or her office labeled "apparel consultant" and charge $100 an hour. Most important is to find someone established and successful in the apparel business who is savvy about issues like advertising and location. This might mean finding a successful store owner in another city or state—one who will not be in direct competition with you—and asking this person to analyze your plans.

Tailor-Made Advice

Rounding out the professional advice triangle will be an honest and experienced lawyer who can take the time to help you with things like zoning, permits, taxes, and vendor contracts, particularly in the start-up phase of your apparel store. And since we're normally talking about lots of money changing hands in this business, you should get an attorney's advice when in doubt about signing papers or reviewing a contract—whether it relates to dealings with your landlord or vendors.

While an accountant's services may not seem as flashy as an attorney's, or even a bona fide business consultant's, believe us, in the apparel business an accountant can have a tremendous impact on your store's bottom line. For example, if you're borrowing money to open your store, your banker will want to see your balance sheet and operating statement, which will be more believable if prepared by someone with the acronym CPA after his or her last name. If you are borrowing less than $500,000, which you will be in this case, most banks will accept unaudited financial statements prepared by a public accountant.

Whether you're opening your store as a sole proprietorship, partnership, or corporation, an accountant can also help during the start-up phase with things like determining the best approaches for your tax situation and internal bookkeeping that will help to keep all your inventory and personnel records straight. In addition, an accountant should take on the less creative aspects of running your apparel store, such as advising you on your overall financial strategy with regard to future purchases and hiring matters.

Where do you find a good accountant? Ask other store owners or your trusted friends, such as those who get a lot of money back from the IRS every year, for recommendations.

The Practice

Hiring an attorney may be the smartest thing you do as an apparel store owner. In general, there are certain apparel-specific situations for which you should always consult an attorney.

- ○ When your store needs to comply with tricky zoning regulations and licensing requirements.
- ○ When you're preparing, negotiating, and executing contracts with your vendors and lessors.
- ○ When you're buying or selling an apparel store.
- ○ When you and/or your business partners are establishing employee relations policies, including hiring, discipline, evaluations, promotions, and terminations.

Your Policy Position

One of the things that will help to balance your daily juggling act will be to establish your store's operating policies, or the rules under which you decide to run your business. It's not until you actually start your own apparel store that you'll realize how many decisions you'll be making on a daily basis, and for that reason we want to make sure you have a plan. Believe us; a plan will eliminate making last-minute reactionary decisions that could result in some costly mistakes, like maybe losing a valued employee. We suggest sitting down and writing up your store's operating policies and supplying copies to your employees. You may also wish to post some of these policies, such as those involving cash and credit card acceptance, for your customers to read.

A seemingly endless number of these policy questions will arise when you enter the apparel business, among them issues surrounding pricing, consignment, purchasing unsolicited products, credit, cash layaway, returns, special orders, damage, children in the store, credit cards, gift wrapping, gift registry, and hours of operation.

We put hours of operation last for emphasis, because when your doors are open will be a big factor in your success. Most apparel stores that don't conform to a mall's shopping hours stay open a minimum of six days per week, usually Monday through Saturday from 10 A.M. to 6 P.M. or 11 A.M. to 7 P.M. Frequently, stores will stay open until 9 P.M. or later on certain, or even several, days of the week, typically Thursday and Friday. Flexible hours allow for lunch-time and evening shopping, and in this business, flexibility is your friend.

Evening hours are crucial in the children's apparel world. Unless you plan to open your store in an affluent area in which stay-at-home moms shop and do lunch while their kids are at day care or in school, your business is most likely to come from households in which there are two breadwinners. Most moms aren't out shopping in the middle of the afternoon anymore, and with more and more mothers also working full or part time, the morning hours aren't as busy as they once were.

This means that more and more children's stores now open at 10 or 11 A.M. and stay open until 7:30 or 8 P.M. to take advantage of evening shoppers. You should also be open on Saturday, maybe even as early as 9:30 A.M.

Layaway

These days, most apparel retailers—including those interviewed for this book—don't offer the standard layaway plan, which entails setting aside merchandise until payments are completed. Mostly this is because a large percentage

Smart Tip

Flexibility is as important in the men's apparel business as it is in the women's business. Why? Because it's mostly women who buy men's clothes.

of consumers make their purchases with credit cards.

If you do decide to offer a layaway plan, be aware of the risks involved. The risky part is that your customer may simply stop making installment payments, and then you're stuck with merchandise you might have been able to sell outright. To guard against problems, put a time limit and minimum deposit on layaways. A 50 percent deposit and 30-day limit are fair. Also consider a nonrefundable fee to compensate for the times you lose a sale.

Returns

Take our word for it. On the first day, if not the first hour, you open your doors, you'll hear the inevitable question: "Can I bring this back if...?" A customer's, or rather a woman's, reasons for wanting to return merchandise will range from the reasonable ("It didn't really match my outfit"; "I should have bought the bigger size") to the my-dog-ate-my-homework excuse ("My mother-in-law doesn't like it"; "My six-year-old daughter wore the shoes to school by mistake").

Men's clothing is not as likely as women's to be returned, because men aren't as fickle about their purchases. And even when we're talking about the overwhelming percentage of women who buy clothes for the men in their lives, these items are not as likely to be returned unless there's a good reason. And returns lessen substantially when it comes to kids clothes. For one thing, a big percentage of kids have no say (literally) in what their parents are buying for them, and even if they can talk, mom still has a big say in what Ryan and Rachel will wear up to, well, maybe the fifth grade.

Obviously, as the store owner, you will decide what's reasonable, and much of your decision will be based on the clothing you sell. "My mother-in-law doesn't like it" won't work for lingerie, for example. Seriously, though, health and hygiene considerations would certainly preclude you from accepting lingerie after it's been worn. All we're saying here is that you need a firm policy in place so that word doesn't spread that you automatically accept returns on undergarments already worn by mothers-in-law.

Still, since superior customer service may be the one thing that separates you from the Gap or Bloomingdale's, you should try to be as liberal as possible on returns. For instance, it may be to your advantage to accept a few unreasonable returns since this often produces the kind of customer loyalty that generates greater sales over the long haul.

"I have a very lenient return policy," says Loeb. "I'll take anything back, no questions asked, unless it's over six months. Even then, I allow customers to make an exchange."

Stat Fact
According to T.J. Reid, author of *What Mother Never Told Ya About Retail* (Retail Resources Publications), less than 5 percent of women's clothes are bought by men.

Special Orders

Bloomies does it, and you might want to consider doing it, too: special orders. Special orders can represent a significant source of income—and instill that loyalty we talked about—since customers are often willing to pay a premium in terms of special shipping, etc., for a specific style, color, or size currently unavailable in the store.

"One of the things my customers love about my store is that they know I'll special-order things," says Loeb. "Every time a customer tries on a jacket or pair of pants that doesn't quite fit, I always offer to get it for them."

As a precaution, you might want to get some kind of a down payment for special orders—like half the retail price—before you place the order.

Gift-Wrapping

Whether or not to offer a gift-wrapping service is another decision you'll need to make. If you run a store with a lot of accessories, like purses and jewelry, it is almost a necessity to provide some form of packaging for gifts. You will find that the costs of attractive wrapping paper, boxes, ribbons, and gift bags are significant, and that wrapping requires a certain amount of skill to create a package that the customer couldn't have otherwise crafted herself.

Fun Fact
According to *Brides Magazine*, the average bride receives an average of $14,000 in gifts. Since there are 2.5 million weddings a year in the United States this translates into a $35 billion market opportunity for wedding gifts alone. Baby showers represent another $20 billion opportunity.

You'll also need to decide whether or not to charge for the service. While most customers are willing to pay, you may opt, in the name of superior customer service, to provide it as a complimentary service rather than charging for it. To minimize costs, you can use craft gift

Children in the Store

Even the Terminator can't destroy your merchandise or delicate store displays like a determined three- or four-year-old can. Parents often don't seem to notice or care that their angel is redressing your mannequins.

To minimize the carnage, and only if space allows it, you might want to consider providing coloring books and crayons (washable) to give those angels an activity. Loeb's, for example, has a corner in the store with toys for the young children of customers. If a child is simply running wild, politely warn the parent that the child might get hurt and hope the parent gets the hint. If not, go straight to plan C: Move stuff out of the Terminator's reach, and pray that the parent remembers that roast in the oven.

bags, on which you could place your store logo and name with an attractive sticker. The bags can then be accented with colorful tissue paper and ribbons or ties.

Purchasing Unsolicited Products

As an apparel store owner, you'll frequently be besieged by sales reps during store hours. In addition, dealing with every peddler—or recognized sales representative, for that matter—can interfere with serving your customers, and you should not hesitate to tell vendors you do not have time to purchase goods during selling hours. Suggest they make an appointment or return when you have help or on a slack day, like Monday afternoon. Even the most persistent sales rep is smart enough to accommodate your busy schedule.

7

A Little
Financial
Footwork

If clothes alone don't make the man—or woman—they certainly don't make the apparel store owner. You can be up on all the latest fashions, drop names of all the hip designers, and schmooze all the right vendors, but if you don't have a business plan in the apparel business, well, let's just say your closet is bare.

As we've said again and again, apparel is a risky business that requires a lot of capital upfront and doesn't often see a return on that investment for the entire first year—if not longer. For those reasons alone, it's important to have a plan in writing that you can refer to in the salad days of your business, something that will remind you of the big picture.

Since it's hard to characterize the apparel entrepreneur—some of you will opt for that expensive corner lot in a busy part of town; others may be located in your local mall—we're going to err on the side of caution when it comes to budgeting, financing, and start-up costs. We are going to recommend that you don't just scribble down some notes on a cocktail napkin, but rather prepare something more formal and official-looking. You will want this basic information down on paper in the likely event that you need to go out to raise capital from investors or get a bank loan.

People get into trouble because they don't know how much their rent should be in ratio to the amount of sales their store is generating. But if reading numbers in columns makes you dizzy, we'll spell it out for you: Rent should be kept between 5 and 6 percent of your total sales, so at the top end, you can figure that you will need $18,000 a year for rent. That means in order to keep rent at 6 percent, your store will have to generate $300,000 in annual sales. Of course, rental rates will vary depending on where you live, so shop around.

Fans of the Plan

The process of creating a business plan forces you to take a realistic, objective, and detached look at your proposed store. It's like therapy, or even a psychic reading—an accurate one, of course—for your business. Why is it important for your apparel store to be "analyzed" or "read"? It's important because most entrepreneurs brainstorming business ideas think they're more clairvoyant than is actually the case.

The whole point of a business plan is to make sure you have both feet planted firmly on the ground. It's one thing to fantasize that your apparel store might someday be featured in *Elle* or *GQ*. It's another to actually have the wherewithal to make it happen. A well-thought-out business plan will not only help you manage your business; it will also help you share your enthusiasm and communicate your ideas to all those mentors and advisors we've been talking about who can potentially lend you money and go to bat for you.

Like a crystal ball—a realistic one, of course—an effective business plan should crystalize your own marketing, financial, and

> **Beware!**
> Think you've got your business plan all worked out in your head and don't need to write anything down? Planning to skip ahead to the next section? Think again. No one will lend you money without a concrete business plan.

buying strategies for running your store, as well as determine your short- and long-term goals, such as whether you would like to break even your first or second year, open two more stores within the next five years or—if you are really aiming high—go global within the next decade.

A textbook business plan for any independent entrepreneur typically has four sections beginning with the "Purpose" or "Summary." This is no different than stating an objective at the top of a resume: "Opening a store that earns $100,000 in revenue annually with the prospect of adding another store in the next five years." (Within your plan, of course, you'll have to say exactly how you're going to clear that kind of cash.) In the summary, you also include your legal form of operation, the amount of the loan you're requesting, and any merchandise, equipment, or fixtures the money will be used for.

> **Tip...**
>
> ### Smart Tip
> Writing an effective business plan isn't easy, nor is it always completely objective or realistic if written in a vacuum (e.g., "My store's going to make $100,000 in the first six months.") We strongly suggest enlisting the help of your mentor or an industry peer.

A table of contents, which you'll probably prepare last, will be inserted next. Then come the four main sections:

1. *Store description*. While we don't recommend that you let your creative juices get out of control, we do want you to be inclusive in your description: "an upscale women's clothing store in a tony suburban neighborhood that specializes in designer eveningwear." This is a start, and to help you fine tune the description, talk to those mentors and business advisors we've so strongly recommended.

2. *Financial data*. This will definitely be trickier than budgeting for that new pair of shoes and will require the help of your mentor, consultant, accountant, and possibly even your attorney. The key financial document will be your profit-and-loss projection (don't worry; that's why you have an accountant) for three years. A P&L is a summary of projected income and expenses, which we'll talk about more in Chapter 14.

3. *Supporting documents*. If you've run other successful businesses in your former life, this is part of your 15 minutes of fame; impressive financial stats will definitely boost your lendability in the eyes of lenders.

4. *SBA materials*. These are relevant only if you want to obtain financing from the Small Business Administration.

It'll Cost You

Yes, opening an apparel store will cost you, and Dr. Stanforth recommends a bankroll of as much as $250,000. But before your heart stops, read on. You can do it for less.

"You may not have $250,000, but my advice is to not even think about opening a store until you've got the right financing," says Waynette Davenport-Ford, a successful Savannah, Georgia, store owner who owns Davenport Designs. As a registered nurse who was eager to get out of the clinical trials business she ran for pharmaceutical companies, Davenport-Ford opened a store featuring unique jewelry, apparel, and gifts in downtown historical Savannah, Georgia, in 1996. "Fortunately, I was able to fund my new venture with the revenue I made from the sale of the clinic," she says. "And during the six years I leased my storefront, I was able to save enough money for the down-payment on the building I'm in now."

It's that common sense factor again that we'll hammer home until you reach the end of this business guide. Clothing store owners can't make it with a fly-by-the-seat-of-your-pants attitude. Besides, it goes against our principle of good business acumen, especially today. Money may not buy love, but it does buy a certain amount of security in this business. "You can't just start a business with X amount of dollars for inventory and hope you sell it," Cohlmia says. "It takes a lot more than that."

Davenport-Ford agrees. "People forget that there is more to worry about than just stocking inventory," she says. "You have to worry about rent, insurance, taxes, and so many other things related to this business."

Minimally—and keep in mind that this information is repeated in Chapters 3, 4, and 12—most entrepreneurs interviewed for this business guide wouldn't dream of opening a store with less than $50,000. Dr. Stanforth recommends $150,000 to get a store up and running, while Debbie Allen, the owner of a Scottsdale, Arizona, women's clothing store and industry speaker, says you should start out with about $100,000 in inventory for a 1,200- to 1,500-square-foot store. Make sure you also plan on enough to get you through a basic build out, marketing plan, and some extra to plan for any mistakes you are making along the way. Many stores fail because they don't plan for enough to get them up and running effectively. The point is, you'll find many conflicting opinions when it comes to the amount of cash you should have to open an apparel store, but we won't get into any trouble by saying the more money you have, the better off you'll be. (Isn't that true in any business?) As Allen says, "The more undercapitalized you are, the longer it will take for you to turn a profit and the less likely it is for you to thrive and grow your business." Now that about says it all.

Tip...

Smart Tip

None of the entrepreneurs interviewed for this business guide was keen on sharing their profit margins. Fair enough. But to give you an idea of what you can expect after your business is up and running, analysts at the investment firm Imperial Capital, indicate that profit margins for apparel retailers range from 4 percent to 13 percent, with average net margins at just below 8 percent. That's not too shabby for a day's work.

Financing Finesse

If you've never done it before, raising capital to start your own business can be a hair-raising experience if you approach it in a haphazard manner. There are several good ways to go about raising money, short of hanging a sign around your neck. You can obviously use your own money, if you have enough sitting in your bank account. You can also bribe others, like friends and family, to lend you the money. Or you can do what thousands of potential small-business owners do every month: You can go to the bank or a small-business investment company and try to arrange financing for a loan.

Now hear this. If there is any single piece of advice we'd like you to leave this chapter with, it's that you'll need to make a careful assessment of just what you're getting yourself into by opening an apparel store. That includes assessing how much capital you're going to need for your particular kind of apparel store and in what increments

Better Banking

Some banks specialize in certain kinds of businesses or have departments that handle specific industries. And, as you've learned here, some banks only go for big money. You can usually tell which banks are interested in attracting loans from small businesses by their eagerness to obtain your account. Here are a few questions to ask your prospective banker that will help you gauge their interest:

❍ Is it necessary to maintain certain balances before the bank will consider a loan?

❍ Will the bank give you a line of credit? If so, what are the requirements?

❍ Does the bank have limitations on the number of small loans it will grant or the types of businesses to which it will grant loans?

❍ What is the bank's policy regarding the size or description of checks deposited to be held for collection?

❍ Will checks under that size be credited immediately to your checking account balance? This is an important question. If you don't have a previous business account to serve as a reference, some banks will hold all checks for collection until they develop experience with you. Whether the bank exercises this precaution may depend on your personal credit rating.

and over what time period. This is where the mentor, consultant, accountant, and attorney—one or all of the above—come in handy. Through this, you'll be better able to assess where that money is going to come from.

Your Own Best Loan

Among entrepreneurs of all stripes, there is one—well, at least one—constant, and that is your best source of financing is yourself. It's the quickest and easiest form of interest-free cash you can acquire, and you won't have to share any of the equity in your business. However, we don't even want to guess at the percentage of you who have access to the large amounts of interest-free cash needed upfront to start an apparel store. Don't despair; read on.

The first people you'll want to target are your friends and relatives, depending on your financial standing with your family and personal support group. If they have the money but are still inclined to run the other way, assure them that the money is a loan and have your attorney draw up papers to verify that. The plus to having those close to you sign legal papers is that it protects the loan and it prevents them from gaining an equity in your store, unless you default on the loan.

Banks might seem like the most likely source of financing, but you should know they are generally the most conservative. Also, most banks will require some sort of collateral as security for the loan, will want to know what the loan is for (that is where the business plan will come in handy), and will also do a background credit check. Depending on the size of the loan, there are several bank loan and collateral possibilities. A savings account, for example, can be used as collateral for a short-term loan. This is actually a good way to get financing, because it lowers your interest rate. For instance, if you take out a loan at 13 percent, and your savings account is earning 7 percent, the actual interest rate you will be paying is 6 percent.

It may also be possible to use your life insurance policy as collateral if it has any cash value. Usually loans can be made up to 95 percent of the policy's cash value. By borrowing against your life insurance policy, you don't have to actually repay the loan; all you really need to do is pay the interest charges along with your premium. However, if you don't repay the amount you borrowed at some time, your life insurance policy will decrease that much in value.

Signature, or personal, loans, which you can take out for several thousand dollars, are a possibility if your credit is good. The drawback, however, is the high interest rates. Another short-term loan is a commercial loan, which is usually issued for a six-month period and can be paid in installments during that time or in one lump sum. Stocks and bonds, your life insurance policy or your personal guarantee can be used as collateral. However, if you are borrowing money to start an apparel store, our guess is that you won't be paying back that loan in six months.

Another option is to use any real estate you own, like your house or condo, as collateral for a loan. Loans like this can be secured for up to 75 percent of the real estate's value and can be set up for a term of 20 years if necessary.

In the apparel business, other loan possibilities include inventory, equipment, and accounts receivable financing. These types of loans have the value of your inventory, equipment, or accounts receivable as security for a loan. Using your inventory as collateral, a bank will usually lend you up to 50 percent of your inventory's value. Equipment loans will cover up to 80 percent of the equipment's value. And with accounts receivable, most banks will loan up to 80 percent of the receivables' value.

Howdy Partner

Using the "strength in numbers" principle, look around for someone who may want to team up with you in your venture. You may choose someone who has financial resources and wants to work side-by-side with you in the business. Or you may find someone who has money to invest but no interest in doing the actual work. Be sure to create a written partnership agreement that clearly spells out your respective responsibilities and obligations so everyone is on the same page.

"Supply-Side" Financing

Although you won't be able to finance your start-up entirely through suppliers, you may be able to offset the cost of the merchandise during your start-up period by obtaining a lengthy payment period, or trade credit. When you're first starting your business, suppliers usually will not extend trade credit because they don't have a history with you. (This is an issue we also touch on in Chapter 11 on merchandising and Chapter 14 on record-keeping.) They're going to want to make all deliveries COD. One of the things you can use as ammunition is a properly prepared financial plan.

If you're successful, you may defer payment for supplies from the time of delivery to 30, 60, or even 90 days—interest free. While this is not specifically a loan, because you don't have to pay for goods right away, the money needed for those supplies is kept in your pocket during the crucial start-up period.

The ABCs of Government Loans

Take advantage of the abundance of local, state and federal programs designed to support small businesses. Make your first stop the U.S. Small Business Administration; then investigate various other programs. Women, minorities, and veterans should check out niche financing possibilities designed to help them get into business. The business section of your local library is a good place to begin your research. So is the internet. One of our entrepreneurs says that in hindsight, it would have been better if she had purchased the facility instead of leasing it, so that she could have applied for an SBA loan.

The Credit You Deserve

Though we wouldn't recommend using your credit cards willy-nilly in the apparel business, it is another way to get start-up capital. Most credit card companies charge extremely high interest rates, but they do provide a way to get several thousand dollars quickly without dealing with paperwork, as long as you don't exceed your limit. If you make sure you use your credit cards as a way to augment your store financing and not as your sole means of raising cash, this can be a viable option.

Overhead

We use overhead here to refer to all nonemployee-oriented expenses required to operate your business. Expenses can be divided into fixed payments made at the same rate, regardless of your volume of business and variable (or semivariable)—those that change according to the amount of business.

- *Fixed expenses.* The best example of a fixed expense is your hypothetical $2,500 rent that must be paid each month. Other fixed expenses are depreciation on fixed assets, like office equipment and computers; staff salaries and other payroll costs; liability and other insurance utilities; membership dues and subscriptions; and any consulting or legal fees.

- *Variable expenses.* The majority of these expenses will include things like your store's advertising and promotional efforts, as well as the price of merchandise, which will fluctuate from month to month. Other variable expenses will include phone calls and office supplies, like cash register tape and any printing, packaging, and mailing related to your advertising and promotional efforts. While these expenses vary from month to month, the total doesn't normally vary greatly from year to year, so you can usually come up with an average figure based on the prior year's total.

The Price Is Right

Establishing fair, competitive prices on all your apparel, figuring appropriate discounts, and arriving at an overall pricing system that allows you to make money can be tricky, especially if you are brand new to the apparel business. We will provide some guidelines, starting with manufacturer recommendations, though we also recommend you do additional research and consult with your own experts.

Most apparel manufacturers will give you a suggested retail price that will range between 100 and 150 percent markup over the wholesale cost they charge you. For example, let's say you buy a T-shirt for $15; you turn around and sell it for $30 and, depending on your competition—or lack of it—even tack on an extra $3 to $4. Doubling the wholesale cost (a 100 percent markup) is known as "keystoning" in the apparel business.

Accessories and specialty items, like candles or maybe hats, are usually marked up 150 to 300 percent over cost, depending on their uniqueness and the market. And purses and jewelry may be marked up 200 to 300 percent, especially if they promise to sell really well (e.g., the t-necklace and butterfly clip craze). You can always put them in the $5 bin later when the craze is over.

Smart Tip

Stale apparel, like stale food, will only rot on your racks. As a rule, a date code should be placed discreetly on each garment's tag indicating the week and month of arrival. No garment should be allowed to hang on the regular price racks for longer than three months. As a common-sense guide, if less than 75 percent of a line sells at a regular price, that line should be discontinued.

Costs of Goods Sold

Cost of goods sold, or cost of sales, refers to your cost of purchasing merchandise from your vendors and suppliers for resale. Freight and delivery charges are customarily included in this figure. Cost of goods sold for an apparel specialty store generally runs close to 60 percent of a store's gross revenue.

Normally, the cost of goods sold bears a close relationship to your store's sales, but it will vary depending on things like whether you're paying more for your merchandise and not offsetting it with a substantially higher retail price, or markup, or if you have a big blowout sale that temporarily inflates your profit margins.

Computing Margin

Gross profit margin, aka gross profit or gross margin, is the difference between your store's net sales (total merchandise sales minus any discounts and/or returns) and the cost of those sales. For example, if Net Sales = $1,000 and Cost of Sales = $300, then Gross Profit Margin = $700.

To make this equation a bit more complex (hint: one for the accountant), gross profit margin can be expressed in dollars or as a percentage. As a percentage, the gross profit margin is always stated as a percentage of net sales. The equation is:

(Total Sales – Cost of Sales) ÷ Net Sales

In the above example, the margin would be 70 percent ($1,000 – $300) ÷ $1,000. For the sake of simplicity, we're assuming total sales and net sales are equal here, without any discounts or returns.

When all operating expenses (rent, salaries, utilities, insurance, advertising, etc.) and other expenses are deducted from the gross profit margin, the remainder is your net profit before taxes. Suffice it to say that if your gross profit margin is not sufficiently large, there will be little or no net profit left. Some businesses, like the apparel business, require a higher gross profit margin than others to be profitable because the costs of operating your store are relatively high.

The following comparison illustrates this point. So that you are not confused, keep in mind that operating expenses and net profit are shown as the two components of gross profit margin—in other words, their combined percentages (of net sales) equal the gross profit margin.

	Store A	Store B
Net Sales	100%	100%
Cost of Sales	40	65
Gross Profit Margin	60	35
Operating Expenses	43	19
Net Profit	17	16

In the first example, the cost of sales (40 percent of net sales) is lower than in the second example (65 percent of total sales), leaving a higher gross profit margin (60 percent vs. 35 percent). But because operating expenses are also higher in the first store (e.g., the Gap), when they are deducted from the gross profit margin, they leave a net profit that's comparable to that of the second store. (While it doesn't hurt to be savvy in the principles of Accounting 101, as we said, this is definitely one for the accountant.)

Computing Markup

Markup and (gross profit) margin on a single piece of merchandise, or merchandise group, are often confused. The reason for this is that when expressed as percentages, margin is always figured as a percentage of the selling price, while markup is traditionally figured as a percentage of the seller's cost. The equation is:

$$(\text{Total Sales} - \text{Cost of Sales}) \div \text{Cost of Sales}$$

Using the numbers from the preceding example, if you purchase goods for $300 and price them for sale at $1,000, your markup in dollars will be $700. As a percentage, this markup comes to 233 percent—($1,000 – $300)/$300. In other words, if your business requires a 70 percent margin in order to show a profit, your average markup will have to be 233 percent.

You can now see from our example that although markup and margin may be the same in dollars ($700), as percentages (233 percent vs. 70 percent), they represent two different things. More than a few new apparel store owners have failed to make their expected profits because the owner assumed that if his markup is X percent, his margin will also be X percent. This is not the case. Again, one for the accountant.

Start-Up Expenses

Since your start-up expenses will differ according to the size and the merchandise volume of your apparel store, look at the sample start-up expenses below as both a low- and high-end guideline. Based on conversations with several apparel entrepreneurs interviewed for this business guide, we're looking at a 1,200-square-foot store with annual gross revenues of around $230,400 on the low end and a 2,000-square-foot store with projected annual gross revenues of $780,000 on the high end. Keep in mind that your own costs will probably be somewhere in the middle.

Expenses	Low	High
Rent (security deposit and first month)	$2,250	$11,700
Initial inventory	$15,000	$35,000
Equipment/fixtures	$5,620	$13,900
Leasehold improvements ($10 to $15 per square foot)	$11,000	$30,000
Licenses/tax deposits	$50	$150
Grand opening advertising	$1,350	$6,000
Utilities/phone deposits	$125	$250
Accounting/legal	$450	$1,350
Owner/operator salary	$1,500	$3,000
Payroll	$2,000	$4,500
Supplies	$500	$1,000
Insurance (first quarter)	$750	$2,100
Miscellaneous	$300	$600
Total Start-Up Costs	**$40,895**	**$109,550**

Start-Up Expenses Worksheet

Here, you can pencil in your own start-up costs.

Expenses

Rent $_____

Initial inventory   _____

Equipment/fixtures   _____

Leasehold improvements   _____

Licenses/tax deposits   _____

Grand opening advertising   _____

Utilities/phone deposits   _____

Accounting/legal   _____

Owner/operator salary   _____

Payroll   _____

Supplies   _____

Insurance (first quarter)   _____

Miscellaneous   _____

_____

_____

_____

TOTAL   _____

Castle burger franchise next to an organic grocery store in Boulder, Colorado. That said, common sense would also suggest that the smart apparel store owner wouldn't dream of opening a women's intimate apparel boutique next to a church or a nursery school.

Presuming you get the drift from these seemingly ridiculous examples, you'd be surprised at the number of businesses—including apparel stores—that fail for precisely this reason: a completely illogical and inappropriate location. But after reading this chapter, there's no way you'd even consider opening Liberal Leisurewear in Kennebunkport.

A Community of Customers

In choosing a community in which to open your store, you'll want to consider a number of location "whether" factors (this will serve as a review of our marketing chapter), including *whether* the community has a large enough population, *whether* its economy is stable enough for you to make money, and *whether* the area's demographic characteristics are compatible with your target market.

In plain English, we'll share even more seemingly ridiculous examples to make our point: Don't open a children's apparel store in a retirement community. Don't open an apparel store in a depressed community where there are few jobs and a huge line outside the unemployment office. Don't open an apparel store in a town where the popu-

Location Logic

Do all the following before you open your apparel store:
- ○ Look at several locations before choosing your store site.
- ○ Check into any local ordinances and zoning regulations that apply.
- ○ Determine your store's parking needs.
- ○ Decide whether the site is worth the rent.
- ○ Define the selling point of your store's location.
- ○ Determine whether the location is an area of potential growth.
- ○ Define your store's space needs.
- ○ Define your store's image.

Location, Location, Location

If you know anything at all about sales, whether it's Buicks, burgers, or bras, you know that location can really make or break your business.

Obviously, you don't want to open a Buick lot in a small farm town where the favored mode of transportation is a tractor or Ford pickup. Nor would you think of opening a White lation is aging such that most people are retired and more likely to spend their Social Security checks on early-bird dinners than clothes. In short, pay attention—particularly to the following advice from several apparel entrepreneurs.

Like many interviewed for this book and possibly many potential store owners studying this business guide, Meridian, Mississippi, store owner Robert Loeb says, "I had the advantage of opening a store in the same town where I grew up. My location research, so to speak, was all through observation of a community with which I was already very familiar." But it was also Loeb's very careful observation that made him open his store in a heavily trafficked downtown area surrounded by mostly male-dominated financial and legal offices, as well as three surrounding hospitals. As he points out, "There are close to 5,000 employees who work within walking distance of my store, and every day the streets are filled with commuters who often make pit stops in my store."

Debbie Allen, the women's store owner and apparel consultant based in Scottsdale, Arizona, adds that entrepreneurs should pay particular attention to foot traffic. Potential green lights are area restaurants that are frequented daily by businesspeople working in the area. "I followed that advice," she says, "and business was really booming until the restaurant next door stopped serving lunch. Then I had to adjust my store hours."

Smart Tip
Tip...

If you are just starting out and aren't lucky enough to have a home-court advantage, Robert Loeb suggests purchasing lists from companies like American Express to see how many people in the community have AmEx cards. He also suggests buying other customized lists. For example, if you're thinking of opening a men's sportswear store, you might want to buy a list from Eddie Bauer and see how many sportsmen you really have in town.

Smart Tip
Tip...

If you're building your own store and are concerned about local zoning regulations, you might want to consult an attorney who can interpret the fine points of the ordinance. There is often a substantial difference between what an ordinance says and the way it is enforced.

And just because you chose the right location for the 1990s doesn't mean it's the best location for the new millennium and beyond. For example, Marcia Sauters, the children's store owner in Santa Monica, has had to relocate her store a couple of times due to increased competition on her street and the skyrocketing rents we talked about earlier. Today she says she can better compete off the beaten path—in her case, a nice area just a mile or so away from the main shopping drag—and with a business that includes more customized accessories. "I'm now in a really cute little 1920s bungalow with its own parking lot," she says. "My shop is probably more of a destination because I don't

Be Community-Conscious

You can learn a great deal about your prospective community by playing detective. In your sleuthing, note the negatives:

○ the necessity for high school and college graduates to leave town to find desirable employment

○ the inability of other residents to find local jobs

○ declining retail sales and industrial production

○ an apathetic attitude on the part of local business owners, educational administrators, and other residents

And the positives:

○ the opening of chain or department store branches

○ branch plants of large industrial firms locating in the community

○ a progressive chamber of commerce and other civic organizations

○ good schools and public services

○ well-maintained business and residential premises

○ good transportation facilities to other parts of the country

○ construction activity accompanied by a minimal number of vacant buildings and unoccupied houses for sale

have a lot of foot traffic. However, I'm right across the street from a preschool and a pediatrician, so it's a great spot for a children's store."

The Clothing Zone

If you locate your apparel store in a building previously used for commercial purposes, such as a bookstore or a coffee shop, you won't have to stress out about things like zoning regulations. However, if you're building your own store, or opening a store in a building that was formerly used as a library or a hospital, you're going to have to check into things like local building and zoning codes to ensure that you're complying with city regulations.

If you don't comply, you may have to file for a zoning variance, a zone change, or a conditional-use permit. A variance or a conditional-use permit will grant you the "conditional" privilege of operating your business on land that is not zoned for that purpose.

A zone change is a permanent change that involves a lengthy procedure of filing petitions with the city and public hearings that aren't much fun unless you like speaking in front of complaining citizens. In addition, there are all sorts of nitpicky things having to do with zoning, such as maximum floor space in relation to land area, maximum heights, and minimum provisions for parking.

It's a Lotta Lease

Signing an apparel store lease requires a heavy financial investment, and if the last decade is any indicator, the price is only going to go up. So now that we've gotten the bad news out of the way, let's get down to brass tacks, or in this case, square feet.

Almost all apparel store lessors, or landlords, require a square foot rental from their lessees, usually paid on a monthly basis. Apparel store rent can run as low as $12 per square foot in certain parts of the country, or as high as $70 per square foot in big malls or shopping centers in high-traffic areas. Higher-rent metropolitan areas across the country, like New York, Los Angeles, Chicago, and Dallas can see rates vary from $60 to $900 per square foot. The per-square-foot charge is usually based on factors such as the size of the area rented (normally renting a very large space entitles you to a somewhat lower charge per square foot, kind of like getting a volume discount), how the space is to be used, the financial reputation of the lessee, and of course, the location.

Lessors, or landlords, sometimes ask for a percentage of the tenant's monthly gross sales—above a certain specified amount—on top of the minimum monthly rental. In a small community shopping center anchored by a large chain drugstore or supermarket, the percentage charge is normally somewhere around 6 percent. Larger regional shopping centers and malls with at least one large department store may charge between 7 and 10 percent of gross sales, depending on the newness of the center, its size, and customer traffic.

In addition to paying flat rents and sales percentages, apparel store owners who decide to locate in a shopping center or mall may be asked to pay what's known as an add-on charge. This per-square-foot charge, or small percentage of a store's gross sales, covers advertising and promotion costs for the shopping area and upkeep of the common areas surrounding the businesses (parking, sidewalk, walkways, sitting areas, patios, restrooms). An apparel store owner

Tip...

Smart Tip

Whatever you do, try to arrange a lease that you can easily hand over to another tenant in the event your store fails or you need to relocate. A provision for subletting to another tenant will let you out of your rental obligation for the balance of the lease and will also allow you to sell your store to a new owner who can assume your lease.

▲

> ## ⚠ Beware!
>
> Occasionally, a site that might be ideal in location and foot traffic may have to be ruled out because the leasing terms are not right for you. Robert Loeb, store owner in Meridian, Mississippi, recommends not getting locked into any kind of long-term lease agreement. He says, "I never signed leases for more than five years in case I wanted to move, which we eventually did after purchasing the building where Loeb's is now located." Whatever you decide, remember all lease terms are negotiable, and the time to negotiate is before you sign on the dotted line.

in a mall may also be assessed a share of the total property tax, based on the square footage of the rented space.

As is the case with any legal document, make sure you carefully read the lease's fine print. Watch out for things like miscellaneous items and administrative expenses. Acceptable "items" include who will pay for any remodeling, any liabilities and duties assumed by you and the landlord, and permission for you to put clothing racks outside during a sale. Sometimes commercial landlords include other clauses in their lease contracts that you might consider, like a bailout clause, which lets you get out of a lease for an agreed-upon reason. Almost all mall leases include charges for maintaining walkways, landscaping, parking lots, and security. Last, but not least, always try to have any renovations made to your store property before you rent. If the landlord won't bear the expense, see if he or she will defer, or waive, the rent for an agreed-upon period of time.

The Right Site: Stopping Traffic

As you have already heard from the entrepreneurs interviewed in this business guide, whether you are opening a women's, men's, or children's apparel store, choosing the right store site within the community is all-important. Just because you open a store doesn't mean they will come.

You'll have to consider your accessibility to customers, your ability to pay the rent, any restrictive ordinances, parking facilities, proximity to other businesses, side of the street—believe it or not—history of the site (not whether or not it's haunted), and terms of the lease, which we've already discussed.

We've also talked about how site costs will vary depending on your store's location. Just as home and condominium prices and rentals fluctuate from coast to coast and from metropolitan areas to smaller towns, you also won't be paying as much per square foot in rural Indiana as you will in, say, midtown Manhattan.

But when considering where to locate, say, your teen-oriented store, don't let cost be the one blinding factor. If, for example, the rent is cheaper on Main Street than in

Movin' on Up

Location, location, location. We used that old cliché about the three most important aspects of real estate as the title of this chapter. But the truth is, while location is a very important part of the apparel business, it may not always be crucial in determining success or failure. Even if your financial circumstances cause you to choose a less-than-ideal location, you can always relocate your store after you're established and you have a better sense of your needs in terms of space and locations.

Often, relocating will not lower your expenses, and the increased sales volume of a better location may at least be partially offset by increased costs. This is especially true of some major shopping mall locations, where rents can be sky-high. Whether locating or relocating, it's always important to look beyond increased sales to the ultimate goal of higher profits.

the Main Mall, but the Main Mall is where the local high school set shops for school clothes, well, it doesn't take a genius to figure out that if you're going to bother opening a store at all, you might as well follow the business. Your anticipated sales volume should more than make things even.

The other thing is scoping out the competition, which we talked about in Chapters 3 and 12. If there are already three teen stores in the Main Mall, you've got a problem that you need to address—either another location or merchandise specialization. And if you can't cater to mall rats by paying mall rents, don't despair. It's all in the foot traffic.

 Beware!
Mall sites, assuming you can find one, require higher rent and start-up costs. You're paying for foot traffic and increased volume.

Aim for Accessibility

Pretend you're in traffic school for a moment and visualize this: If your store is located on a four-lane road with a median divider, traffic on the far side of the street will not have easy access to your store unless you're on the corner where left-hand turns are permitted. If traffic is often heavy and congested, or if the speed of traffic is more than 35 mph, people may find your store more of a hassle than a convenience. Also, narrow entrances and exits, turns that are hard to negotiate, and

⚠ Beware!

While two car dealerships or two department stores may be able to compete side by side, the same can't be said of children's or men's clothing stores since they draw most of their customers from the immediate area.

parking lots that are always full are deterrents—not to mention great incubators for road rage.

If you depend a lot on pedestrian traffic, the distance of your site from other locations generating customers and/or employees is also important. In a downtown shopping district or in a shopping center, for example, where a major retailer is the chief traffic generator, the farther you are from that store, the less accessible your business will be to pedestrians. Even your entrance can be an accessibility factor. If it's above street level or on an upper floor, or if access can be gained only from a side street, you may want to consider another site.

We suggest you spend several weekdays and weekends analyzing your intended site, which is no different from checking out the neighborhood where you are considering buying a house. Analyze the site's accessibility and whether it generates more foot or car traffic due to its location. Sit in your own car and gauge foot and car traffic patterns at different times of the day to see if they coincide with your intended store hours. (You'll want to conduct this same test after you've actually opened your store's doors to see whether those hours need adjusting.) Watch to see if people look confused as to where to find the store's entrance.

Also check out the kinds of people you see driving and walking around your potential store site. Are these the kind of people who are likely to be shopping for your clothes? You might even want to get out of your car and try a little guerrilla marketing tactic of conducting some man-on-the-street interviews. Do people feel a need for a children's clothing store in this location? Or are they strictly mall devotees? Would they be interested in buying what you're selling?

Plausible Parking

With the increase in shopping center crime, particularly in parking lots and parking structures, parking safety is a big deal these days. Because of this, in addition to adequate parking, you will want to make sure your store provides a parking lot that is well-lit, and if need be, has a security guard. During your site analysis, you will also have to consider the condition of the

Bright Idea

All our talk about customer service and unique clothing aside, the prime location for a men's store is still a large shopping mall, where men might go to see a movie or shop for sporting goods.

parking area and whether or not it needs expansion or resurfacing. We don't care how nifty your clothes are. If customers get a flat tire every time they sink into one of your lot's potholes, they will be shopping elsewhere.

Proximity to Other Businesses

Your neighbors as well as your potholes may influence your sales volume. There are plenty of studies of natural clusterings of businesses showing that certain businesses do well when located close to one another. For a children's clothing store, customers who patronize such places as toy stores, health clubs with day-care centers, grocery stores, restaurants, pizza parlors such as Chuck E. Cheese's, candy shops, and malls are also prospects for your business. As Scottsdale, Arizona, apparel entrepreneur Debbie Allen mentioned earlier, a woman's clothing store often thrives best in commercial areas where professional women—with money—can shop during their lunch hours or immediately after work.

Which Side of the Street?

No, this is not an old wives' tale. The sunny side of the street is generally less desirable for retail operations than the shady side, especially in warm climates. In fact, research shows rents to be higher on the shady side of the street in upscale shopping areas and that apparel merchants recognize the sunny side of the street principle by installing awnings to make customers more comfortable.

Retailing research has also shown that the "going home" side of the street is usually preferable to the "going to work" side (another thing to analyze as you sit in your car watching traffic). And it only stands to reason; people have time to stop at your store on the way home, not when they're in a hurry to get to work on time, which is something else to keep in mind if you think you should open your store at 8 A.M. just because you are a "morning person."

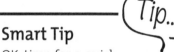

Smart Tip

OK, time for a quick review on the finer points of store location. Think foot traffic. Think upscale open-air shopping center or commercial district attracting many browsers during lunch hours, evenings, and weekends. Think accessibility.

History of the Site

You should learn the recent history of any potential store site before making a decision. Most Americans no longer believe in haunted houses, but experienced apparel retailers know that "jinxed" locations exist. These can be stores in malls and big shopping centers, as well as independently located stores that have repeatedly been business failures. However, the reason for one or several businesses failing in a given site may be completely unrelated to the success potential of your clothing store. A mall that was once a washout may now be anchored by Nordstrom; a once-dead street may now be a gentrified yuppie mecca. As we mentioned earlier, you'll want to determine the reason for previous failures to see if you can avoid them.

Common and Community Sense

By now, there's no way you'd ever consider opening an intimate apparel store next to a nursery school. Or Liberal Leisurewear in Kennebunkport, Maine. Or any of the other obviously bad examples we made throughout this chapter. They did all have a point, however, and that is that you need to know your community, like your merchandise, inside and out.

Casting Call
Hiring Employees

Finding good sales help for your apparel store can often be like, well, finding a Donna Karan suit for $100—difficult, but not impossible, if you know where to look. In this chapter, we're going to "help" you do just that: find motivated—even career-oriented—salespeople who can cheerfully fold clothing, chat up customers, and move your merchandise right out the door.

Starting Solo

Hiring may not be something you think about right away. Unless you've got a lot of extra money to throw around after buying inventory and promoting your store (which we'll get into in Chapter 13), you might want to run things yourself or with your price-is-right spouse until your store becomes somewhat established. However, once that foot traffic picks up speed and the customer line is out the door on Saturday afternoons, you'll need to think about hiring at least part-time help. And thinking ahead, you may even need a store manager to hold down the fort when you take a well-deserved day off.

Aside from a store manager, you'll need clerks. We know; the standard image of an apparel store clerk, usually working at a mall chain store, is a surly, gum-chewing student whose parents have forced her to get a summer job. They're more motivated to stand at the cash register and gossip about their weekend than to help your customers find their sizes or help make your business more profitable.

At least that's the image. The reality, according to the apparel entrepreneurs we interviewed, is much different—if you know where to look.

To boil it all down, while your needs will vary according to your store hours and customer traffic, a good rule of thumb is one full-time and one part-time person for a 1,000-square-foot store.

Not a Burger Background

When hiring sales staff, sales ability and personality come first. With both of those traits upfront, you can always train your salespeople to track inventory and handle apparel. Ideally, with that combination, your salespeople will also be able to deal with the everyday apparel pressures of customer personalities and demands that require a thoughtful combination of tact, persuasiveness, and a sense of humor. You also want a person who is mature and honest, one who will not only help you move merchandise out the door but also one you trust to handle your cash and to keep careful and complete records.

"You obviously have to be particular about who you hire," says Meridian, Mississippi, entrepreneur Robert Loeb, "because ultimately

> **Bright Idea**
> Depending on your inventory, you might also hire a part-time seamstress to handle alterations, either in your store or out of their home. And depending on your sales volume, you might want to follow the lead of store owner Robert Loeb, who has a full-time seamstress.

it's customer service that separates us from the mall stores. In my store, as is the case with many of my peers, we keep a book with our customers' names, as well as their spouses' and children's names. In this book we also keep track of the kind of merchandise they buy, along with their clothing likes and dislikes.

"So foremost, you need people who are willing to develop a rapport with your customers, those who are both willing to shake hands with and remember your customers by name every time they come in. No salesperson should be afraid to pick up the phone and call a customer when merchandise comes in that they might be interested in seeing. Of course, it's also helpful for people to either have apparel knowledge or a strong desire to learn about the business."

In short, whether your needs require you to hire a younger (say if you're opening a surf shop) or bit more "mature" employee (if you're opening a women's haute couture store), you should rule out the sales associate of the month from the local McDonald's drive-thru, since, in the apparel business, there's more to the job than just waiting for customers to show up. Besides the ability to deal with customers and cash, any kind of apparel experience, whether we're talking fabrics or inventory control, is

> **Tip...**
>
> ### Smart Tip
> As a rule of thumb, you don't want to hire a male sales associate in a woman's clothing store, but you can hire a woman to sell in a men's clothing store. Why? Simple, according to author T.J. Reid: "Men don't buy women's clothes, so they probably wouldn't be the best choice to sell them, but since women do buy men's clothing, they'll know what they're talking about in a men's store."

Building Your Dream Team

The more educated and inspired your sales staff is, the better they will be at their jobs. It's as simple as that. Start by teaching your staff the basics and what's unique about your store. When employees reach a level where the excitement of the new job may have worn off and some staffers may even be frustrated because they see other team members making all the sales, be the store cheerleader. Encourage your staff to ask questions. Teach them how to continue their after-sale service by sending out thank-you cards or making personal calls to see how the customers are enjoying their purchases. Encourage them to start building their own client call lists. Delegate them to areas where they show special strength. Show your appreciation and reward employees for their sales accomplishments. Empower your staff, and you'll make more money.

a plus since you may need some additional input when it comes to dealing with clothing manufacturers and sales reps.

Teaching Sales Tactics

Even a part-time sales clerk who's been taught a little basic selling savvy can take a customer who came in for a pair of socks and sell him or her—or at least show him or her—a shirt or other "necessary" accessory. The trick is knowing how to teach and hone that savvy in such a way that your salespeople remain just that—salespeople, and not predators.

You may wonder why teaching is even necessary, particularly if you're an apparel store owner who has gone out of your way to hire someone with apparel experience. The truth is, all bosses (that's you in this case) in every office, even if we're talking about 50 bank credit offices, have their own personal style and ideas of how things should be done; since people aren't mind readers, these ideas need to be clearly passed on to every employee hired. The added bonus in the apparel business as opposed to, say, a bank credit office, is that the better-trained your salespeople are, the more they'll contribute to your personal overall profits.

So even if your bright and personable new salesperson spent last summer selling makeup at the mall, you'll want to teach them the basics of your store. This doesn't mean hovering, however. According to retail expert Debbie Allen, you're going to ultimately want to let your salespeople develop the skills of greeting your customers on their own without watching their every move. When you give your salespeople some leeway, you're allowing them to develop their own rapport with customers, which will ultimately build their confidence on the sales floor.

Allen also stresses, "Treat your staff as if they were customers in your store, selling them on the excitement of your inventory, so they can pass that excitement on to your customers." Take the time to walk your employees through your inventory lines and the most popular items, explaining why your customers value these items. Your salespeople will increase their sales—and your bottom line—dramatically when they have genuine enthusiasm for the clothes they're selling. According to Allen, they'll also do a better job and increase sales

> **Bright Idea**
> It's a good idea to hold regular staff meetings, during which employees can discuss any problems and also be encouraged to offer input, whether it's new merchandising ideas or possible store promotions. This way, even if your employees are part-timers, they'll still feel like a part of your team and not just someone doing unappreciated grunt work to pay their way through school.

when that enthusiasm and motivation are rewarded (more on that later in this chapter under "Personnel Perks").

Finding the Right Fit

Recruiting employees for your apparel store, like other small businesses that tend to hire mostly part-time help, will be limited by geography—your employees may not have their own cars, for example—as well as the fact that their employee discount might be better put to use at the Gap down the street.

Taking these factors into consideration, how do you find qualified employees? First off, like any smart employer, you're going to write down a job description that includes all "sales" responsibilities, including any physical requirements of the job, such as unpacking boxes and vacuuming when necessary. That said, you're not going to want to waste any time advertising at the local fashion merchandising school if you're just looking for a strong, healthy teen to help you lift boxes in the storeroom.

But, as you've probably gathered by our earlier fast-food examples, if you are in need of experienced help, you will have to take some sort of proactive recruiting approach. If your store merchandise warrants a stylish, youthful image, you'll want to go out and recruit at local colleges and universities that have fashion merchandising programs. These schools will likely have job placement bureaus as well as bulletin boards, where students will be looking for work in their chosen field of study. If you're merely looking for "help," you might also want to ask for referrals from trusted friends, whose daughters or sons may need part-time work while home from school, during the summer, or holidays. Placing classified ads in local newspapers can also work, particularly if you're looking for more mature part-time help.

Author T.J. Reid advises, "Since most specialty shops are open 9 to 5 or 6, with the early hours usually the slowest, why not hire extra people just for the busy lunch hour?

You Heard It Here First

According to studies conducted by apparel experts, the five things customers liked least in a sales clerk were: insincere flattery, overstaying their welcome, too much talking, not keeping promises, and arguing. The five things they liked the most were: product knowledge, presentable appearance, courtesy, honesty, and sincerity.

There are many mothers with children in preschool who would love to work just three hours a day. Plus, there are the schoolteachers who get off at 3 P.M. and could supplement their incomes with a part-time job from 5 to 7. If you find these special people with special needs, you'll discover faithful employees who don't need all the extra benefits of retirement, vacation, and sick leave."

According to Reid, newspaper ads are a great place to solicit these special people. However, if you're not in a big hurry to hire anyone and would prefer to take a more passive approach, simply place a help wanted sign in your store's front window. Over the years, thousands of apparel store owners—including a few interviewed for this business guide—have found help that way, and guess who more often than not turned out to be their best recruits? You got it: devoted customers turned devoted salespeople.

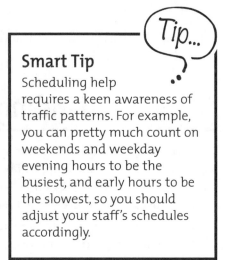

Smart Tip

Scheduling help requires a keen awareness of traffic patterns. For example, you can pretty much count on weekends and weekday evening hours to be the busiest, and early hours to be the slowest, so you should adjust your staff's schedules accordingly.

Sales Security

Whatever recruitment methods you use, you'll need to determine how reliable and trustworthy the applicant will be as an employee. Does the 20something college student have a heavy load of classes that requires her to leave early often? Did she mention that she also has a part-time job bartending at an after-hours club? Did the mother of two mention that she has a hard time keeping a full-time babysitter? These might seem like commonsense questions, and they are; we just want to make sure you ask them before it's too late. It's also important that your salespeople, even part-timers, are compatible with you and other salespeople in your store. Remember, employees don't have the luxury of going into a private office where they can shut the door and chill out. You are in constant contact with each other for many hours at a time and should be the model of good behavior for your customers. Our point here: With each applicant, check references and conduct an extended interview with pointed questions, even if that applicant is your friend's daughter or son.

Beware!

. . . of "shrinkage," an apparel industry term that refers to employee theft. Hopefully, you'll have made wise choices in the employee department and the only shrinkage you'll have to worry about will have to do with those jeans you sell.

A Super Sales Clerk

On the fence about one of your current sales clerks? She'll need to score heavily in the "yes" column on this test borrowed from *The Salesmanship Guide* (Darnell Industries). Need we say more?

		Yes	No
1.	Can she make effortless small talk to put customers at ease?	❏	❏
2.	Does she try to find out the customer's needs before trying to make a sale?	❏	❏
3.	Does she establish professionalism and expertise without sounding like a know-it-all fashion maven?	❏	❏
4.	Does she demonstrate warmth that shows she truly cares about the customer and how he or she looks?	❏	❏
5.	Does she show customers that your store guarantees and stands behind the garments it sells?	❏	❏
6.	Does she always make sure customers are aware of credit, exchange, and other store policies to avoid misunderstandings?	❏	❏
7.	Does she demonstrate that your merchandise and prices are the best available for the customer's selection in the area?	❏	❏
8.	Is she willing to take no for an answer and leave customers alone if they can't make up their minds?	❏	❏
9.	Can she show customers, without emotion, why they should make their purchase at your store?	❏	❏
10.	Do your customers refer others to your store?	❏	❏

To Commission or Not to Commission

Try to keep salaries in line with your competition—or better, if you can. While wages depend heavily on the cost of living and the prevailing wage in your area, these days most beginning full-time salaries in the apparel business range from minimum wage in small-town apparel stores to minimum wage times two in larger metropolitan areas. Just like corporate employers, you'll want to have a merit system of pay raises in place, at least for any full-time employees, so that employees can be rewarded after a good annual review.

Testing Your Tolerance

Just call it the Myers-Briggs test for apparel entrepreneurs, which we, in fact, borrowed from *How to Start and Run Your Own Retail Business* (Carol Publishing Group). In our test, you'll want to be sure you're an ENFP: Extroverted Natty Fashionable People-person.

The successful manager of a small apparel store:

○ must be strongly motivated and want to get ahead

○ prizes independence

○ has the ability to "read" customers—to determine and satisfy their needs

○ gets along well with other people

○ has a sympathetic ear and tries to understand others and their situations

○ has a sense of fairness

○ has the ability to adapt to change

○ is inquisitive, imaginative, innovative, perceptive, and decisive

○ is able to inspire and direct employees

○ is willing to serve the people with whom he or she deals and the community as well

Though many apparel chain stores operate on some kind of commission basis, it's not necessarily the case among smaller, independent stores. Talk about predators. Though it depends on the size of the store, sales volume, and how many people you have working for you, most apparel experts agree that a traditional commission structure tends to encourage rivalry among the sales ranks, which is the last thing you need as you try to develop an honest and helpful rapport with customers.

As author T.J. Reid says, "Commissions tend to cause dissension and high-pressure sales tactics, especially if you only have two employees. The two will kill each other get-

Dollar Stretcher

There are government programs available to help you train and hire new personnel. The Working for America Institute (WAI) has a variety of action briefs, brochures and checklists for employers available online at: www.working foramerica.org.

ting to a customer and in the end will care more about how much money is being made from the sale instead of whether they have made the right merchandise match."

If you're dead set on offering your employees some kind of a commission structure, conduct a survey among your peers and you'll more than likely learn that these days most apparel-related commissions being paid are on a group basis. This way, a bonus is paid to all employees if the store meets or exceeds sales goals. Also, if the store outperforms a prior year's or month's sales figures, employees can be rewarded based on a percentage of that increase.

Personnel Perks

Many of those who work in clothing stores do it for the convenience, fun of it, clothing discounts, and maybe even the prestige of being a fashion consultant—not for the money.

For that reason, many apparel store owners offer their employees other kinds of perks, like maybe an annual all-expenses paid trip to a convention of their choice, a year-end bonus, or a discount on store merchandise. According to author T.J. Reid, the standard employee discount has risen from 25 percent to around 40 percent. Some highly successful store owners even offer 50 percent employee discounts.

Never a Dull Moment

Having a slow sales day? Take it from author T.J. Reid and try out new store displays. Play what Reid calls "match up," where employees take turns coordinating difficult outfits. Another idea if traffic is sparse is to have each of your employees call five customers and give them the lowdown on the latest arrivals. If one of these customers comes into the store within three days, offer a small cash reward, whether the customer makes the purchase or not. Near holiday times, you can also use slow hours to address envelopes for your after-holiday sale.

Not a Diamond in the Rough

The moral of our personnel chapter is this: A good staff is probably easier to find than a discounted Donna Karan suit. And if you treat your staff right, it will pay off in more ways than one.

Beware!

At the federal level, employee safety and health are regulated by provisions of the Occupational Safety and Health Act of 1970 (OSHA). In retail establishments, the most often repeated violations are improperly marked or unmarked exits, fire extinguishers not mounted and/or not easy to spot when needed, and fall-hazard debris in storerooms.

Dressed for Success

Setting Up Your Store

There's no need to hit the panic button when it comes to buying equipment for your apparel store. First off, your major purchases won't require any superhuman knowledge of high-tech equipment that's hard to pronounce or demands expensive upgrades. In fact, a lot of this stuff you'll be able to get used, but more on that later.

Second, considering that your rent and merchandise will be costly—and barring an expensive Elle Decor-like interior design—you also won't have to worry about forking over huge outlays of money for things like hanging rods, dress racks, mannequins, and shelving.

Breathing Room

On the one hand, you'll want your store to be spacious and uncluttered, in keeping with the uncluttered trend in merchandising today, which we'll cover in greater depth in Chapter 11. On the other hand, you will definitely not want to be "Lost in Space." And there are very good reasons for not having enough room to hold a yoga class in the middle of your store. One that we've already discussed is the fact that over the past decade or so, commercial rents for apparel store owners have gone way up, even quadrupled in areas like Southern California. Also, just like your house, you're going to have to furnish all that space with either fixtures or merchandise.

"Most first-time store owners get into spaces that are too big," says Lee Leonard, a partner with New York City-based marketing and consulting company D.L.S. Outfitters. "They think all that space is impressive and looks good, which it does. The only problem is you've then got to fill it with merchandise, which financially you might not be prepared to do."

While most apparel entrepreneurs interviewed for this guide said 1,200 to 1,500 square feet was the average and sometimes ideal amount of space needed for a specialty store, size obviously differs. Debbie Allen started out with only 900 square feet 20 years ago, when rent was a mere $8 per foot (it still can be in some parts of the country). But because she's been so successful over the years, she learned how to be comfortable running a 4,000-square-foot store and multiple locations by learning how to put systems in place.

Finesse with Fixtures

In the apparel world, fixtures mean more than nifty brass lights and quaint knobs you can find at specialty hardware stores. Here, in addition to lighting, fixtures include a long list of things needed for merchandise display: partitions, paneling, signage, storage shelves and/or cabinets, checkout counter(s), tables, stands, wall units, showcases, and mannequins.

Dollar Stretcher

Most apparel store owners buy new fixtures, such as lights and clothing racks, and you can usually find great deals in so-called fixture houses near your local apparel mart.

The Final Word on Fixtures

In general, you probably will be smart to spend whatever is necessary to buy new or new-looking fixtures to give your store the modern, contemporary look so popular today. But because start-up costs are high, you may want to cut corners where you can. Some manufacturers supply free display fixtures with a specific minimum order of merchandise. Others offer low prices for fixtures that will display only their products. Ask your inventory suppliers about such arrangements and the terms of availability.

Another way to save on store fixtures is to buy from store closeouts or from retailers/private parties who sell used store fixtures. Discounts for used items can run up to 50 percent. Look in your local newspaper classifieds and Yellow Pages.

The cost of these fixtures really depends on your store's location, its size, and the kind of merchandise you'll be selling. The cost also depends on the type of image you want to project, and whether you'll be using new or used fixtures.

Assuming that your taste will be somewhere in between Saks and Sears, average figures from a variety of apparel retailers show you should plan on spending at least $10 per square foot,

Dollar Stretcher

If you want to purchase pre-owned fixtures, you can check out your local liquidators, which carry all kinds of leftover fixtures from stores that have recently gone out of business.

but, again, the price can easily be doubled or tripled depending on your store's location and size. If you fancy yourself a home improvement kind of store owner, you will no doubt save yourself plenty of money in the process. And even if you are no handyman, you could probably cut your square-foot cost by finding yourself a handy friend who can help you put up shelves or hang hooks or pegboards for wall displays.

Another cost-saving tip: If you want an Elle Decor design but are operating on a Sears budget, you might consider combing your local flea market, where you can get great deals on eclectic furniture, lamps, and other items that can be used as store "fixtures."

Checkout Counter

It may not be the most fashionable fixture in your apparel store, but it's where the money will be changing hands, so let's start with the checkout counter. In general, the checkout counter at most specialty apparel stores is a split-level counter—the higher level for the customer, the lower level for you and your employees—that is generally anywhere from 5 to 8 feet long. You can figure a height of about 45 inches on the customer's side, which is usually a thin ledge on which they can place their purchases and cash and/or plastic. A counter of about 36 inches on the sales clerk's side provides a working surface for running the cash register, wrapping items, and writing out sales slips. Shelves under the counter provide space for storing business forms, receipts, and other miscellaneous supplies. If you have a split-level counter built from the floor up, it can cost you anywhere from $200 to $1,000, depending on the style and materials.

Cash Registers—to ECR or Not to ECR

The most important fixture on your checkout counter will be a good electronic cash register (ECR). In case you haven't noticed, cash registers have come a long way since the old ring-dinging dinosaur models you used to see in old TV sitcoms. Today, there are whole integrated Point of Sale (POS) systems that are networked through a computer, the kind of state-of-the-art system ideally suited for a multi-checkout store or a multi-chain operation (in other words, worth knowing about but maybe not the kind of high-tech gadget you'll need to invest in right away). Anyway, for future reference, each POS terminal is a complete checkout center with a cash drawer, magnetic strip reader for credit card verifications, scanner for UPC codes, receipt printer, 32-button keyboard, and a customer display monitor. You can even program your checkout system so that sales and other information can be logged instantly onto your computer. It also allows you to receive sales data immediately so that management reports can be produced, inventory levels updated, and product lines tracked more efficiently.

As we said, the big question here is do you need such a complicated system for your own apparel store, at least in the beginning? At a cost of around $1,200 to $5,000 for each terminal, it's doubtful you'll want to spend that kind of money during your start-up period. Instead, the best option for the small apparel entrepreneur is an electronic cash register. Starting as low as $600 and going as high as $3,000, many new ECRs offer a variety of options, such as payment records to designate a cash, check, or charge purchase; department price groupings; sign-in keys to help managers monitor cashiers and clerks; and product price groupings to track inventory more effectively.

> **Bright Idea**
>
> Check on a lease-purchase arrangement for your ECR; this will run about $100 to $150 per month. You can also lease a mechanical cash register in your early phase and decide what to buy later.

ECRs perform several bookkeeping functions and can track inventory and customer accounts. Still, there are some apparel retailers who believe that an ECR or any cash register is an invitation to thieves, as well as a significant expense. If you don't buy or lease a cash register, you can get by with an adding machine with tape and a cash box—it'll cost $50 to $200 for the adding machine and $25 to $40 for the cash box—but this is a very unsophisticated way to go, and we don't really recommend it.

Mannequins

Mannequins are typically the most logical way to display your clothing, not to mention a fun way to indulge in a kind of adult dress-up game. The shoppers' mindset assumes happy faces equal happy places and if they see interesting, dynamic mannequins, they assume the store and its staff are also interesting and dynamic.

Although still favored by some retailers, the 1950s Barbie doll style mannequins are not used as often these days. Clothiers can now choose from a variety of styles that enhance their store's theme. Some mannequins are headless or faceless or all one color. You can find some made out of translucent fiberglass, fabric or wood, while others look like a cartoon character with pink swirled hair. Today's trend also finds mannequins in casual poses like sitting, walking, or reclining, or actively posed to run or skate.

However, mannequins can be expensive—anywhere from $125 to $600 for a really deluxe model mannequin. Another consideration that author T.J. Reid points out is, "Besides being expensive, the problem with mannequins is that because styles change so quickly, a mannequin's hair and makeup can also become quickly outdated." Fortunately, there are alternatives that can still make an impression on window shoppers.

Instead of mannequins, many apparel shops, even major department stores, now use wire display forms or headless T-stands to display their clothing, which can be purchased at the fixture houses mentioned earlier. Shop owners featuring infant wear often use life-size baby dolls to display layette outfits. If you have a lot of wall space, you can attach or hang garments on them.

Most importantly, keep in mind that it's not necessarily what you use to display garments, but how you display them. Lucia Luis, Senior Account Executive for Window-Mannequins, says that you need to do more than put a mannequin in your store window to

Dollar Stretcher

Obviously, bags are necessary for your customers' purchases. In the beginning, get plain, undecorated bags, which usually come in bales of 500 and, depending on the size and strength, can cost $5 to $20 per bale.

having an eye-catching display. "The keys to creating an effective window display are lighting, props, and colors," he says. "It is both possible and simple to build an attractive display on any budget."

Tip...

Smart Tip
Always remember that you want space-saving fixtures that enable you to display the most merchandise in the smallest amount of space.

Tables

In general, we don't recommend that you display merchandise by stacking it on tables because it gives that "blue light special" appearance we talked about earlier. However, you may need tables for hats or T-stands that will be displaying accessories like hats and jewelry, or even sale items. And like we said earlier, flea markets are a great place to find unique and inexpensive tables.

Hangers

They may not be the most exciting pieces of equipment you buy—or the ones that customers look at first—but, nonetheless, hangers are an essential display item. There are two basic hanger styles. One is a simple hanger for blouses, sweaters, shirts, and dresses. The other is a wishbone type, which has a hanging rod across the bottom and may come equipped with clothespins. Use hanging rods for things like suits and coordinated separates, draping or pinning slacks across the bottom rod. Believe it or not, hangers—plastic, not wire—are expensive, so buy them in bulk at volume prices. In addition, you'll probably need a few hundred assorted plastic size dividers to separate your merchandise on the racks.

If you give away hangers with each purchase, go ahead and get the lightweight kind, which will cost between 25 and 30 cents apiece. Heavy-duty plastic hangers can cost as much as 50 cents apiece, so if you splurge, you might not want to let your customers take these out of the store.

And FYI: Cheaper, more lightweight plastic hangers tend to break easily and become brittle in cold weather. Since you'll be buying in bulk, which will cut down on the cost, you might want to invest in more expensive hangers.

Clothing Racks

Clothes racks for the display floor come in circular, S-shaped, three-sided and various other configurations, and in various materials ranging from chrome to wood.

Frequently, clothes racks can be bought from the same companies that supply hangers (see Appendix). Typically, these companies will also supply you with pricing equipment and related items. You can luck into great bargains on racks. Double-chrome racks can cost up to $200 each, but at a closeout sale, an auction, or a used-goods dealer, you may be able to get good-quality racks at half-price or less.

You will need clothes racks against the wall, too. Many handyman-type store owners build these themselves, using wood such as redwood, cedar, or fir for the frame and hanging a small-bore galvanized pipe the length of the frame. Now, if you're just not in the home improvement frame of mind, new wall racks can run anywhere from $45 to $60 apiece new.

Lighting

Every apparel retailer wants his or her store to sparkle and shine, and for customers to take note of their merchandise rather than the shelves and racks on which it's displayed. Every smart apparel retailer also knows that the store's lighting should be as flattering to the customer as it is to the merchandise.

A store's lighting depends a lot on its size and design, the age of the building, the available natural light, and the brightness desired by the apparel store owner. The basic types of lighting available are fluorescent, incandescent, and neon. Incandescent lighting, which is closest to natural lighting, is generally best, and a word to the wise here: If you're opening a women's apparel store and you want women to buy anything at all after trying on clothes, forget fluorescent or neon lighting in your dressing rooms.

Ticketing Machines

There are many different models of ticket-making machines that you might find useful. The most deluxe models, which run around $300, allow you to add price tags to garments using your own codes, which can really help you with inventory control. Some ticketing systems even tie into that ECR system we talked about.

You can also obtain clothing tickets—those plastic clamps—that can only be removed with a special device you'll keep at the checkout counter. These special tickets will trigger alarms if a tagged garment is removed from the store and will also release a staining blue ink if removed without the special device. Tickets can be a deterrent to shoplifting.

Equipment Accessories

Most entrepreneurs find a trip to the local office supply store just as much fun as visiting the mall. It's easy to get carried away when you're surrounded with an abundance of clever gadgets, all designed to make your life easier. But if, like most new business owners, you're starting on a budget, discipline yourself to get only what you need. Do comparison shopping online, as well as at warehouse stores, chain stores, and other suppliers to be sure you're getting the best price, quality, and service package.

Some types of office equipment you'll need to outfit your store may include:

- *Telephone.* Two telephone lines should be adequate during the start-up period with the option to add additional lines if needed. You may also want to consider having a toll-free number so that customers won't have to think twice about calling you to place an order.

- *Answering machine or voice mail.* Your business phone should never go unanswered, even when the store is closed.

- *Cell phone.* You should always be available to employees, especially if questions arise concerning a customer or vendor or other concerns.

- *Credit and debit card processing equipment.* This could range from a simple imprint machine to an online terminal. Credit and debit card service providers are widely available, so shop around to understand the service options, fees, and equipment costs. Expect to pay about $500 for a "swipe" machine that reads the magnetic strip on cards. You'll also pay a transaction charge, which might be a flat rate (perhaps 20 to 30 cents) per transaction or a percentage (typically 1.6 to 3.5 percent) of the sale.

- *Fax machine.* Very helpful when dealing with vendors and suppliers.

- *Photocopier.* This equipment is a fixture of any business and can be very useful even to the smallest company.

- *Paper shredder.* A necessary item in a growing concern for privacy issues.

- *Postage meter and scale.* You'll need these if you offer shipping as a perk.

- *Other incidentals.* These may include a calculator, stapler, calendar, rolodex, and tape dispenser.

Computer

I'll bet you thought we forgot about this little gem—the computer. However, it may be the most expensive, yet most underused piece of equipment in an apparel store.

According to author T.J. Reid, "The more seasoned the apparel retailer, the more likely they are to be using computers in their store. However, the truth is that most apparel retailers aren't that computer-savvy. They might have a computer at home, but in their stores they're still using some kind of manual bookkeeping device."

In an ideal world, a computerized record-keeping system can help you keep track of expenses, inventory, and customer records. And if you're worried about money, don't think that you need a fancy, color-coordinated computer to match your outfits (Apple's iMac, however, is both cute and affordable at less than $2,000). You can dress up your store with the technological basics: 64MB of RAM, a 1 GB hard drive, a VGA monitor, and internet access.

As far as software goes, Best Software's ACT! does general bookkeeping, payroll, and receivables. It runs around $220. Accpac by Simply Accounting will walk you through basic accounting principles. Accpac Inventory Control is a basic inventory system. It runs $275 to $350. Quickbooks for Windows will do invoicing, payroll, accounts receivable, employee records, and keep up-to-date tax information. It runs $180 to $500. PeachTree Complete or their One-Write Plus software provides complete accounting and inventory listing systems. It runs $100 to $300.

Varying Technological Tastes

Whether you or your accountant is doing the math, you can both get help from any number of apparel-specific software programs on the market today. And believe us, if you do decide to do your own math, there isn't an accountant in the world who wouldn't advise you to use any number of the prepackaged programs available to you today. True, the following are sophisticated and more expensive—a few hundred dollars at the least—financial packages that will probably be used more by a large store owner or apparel chain owner, but you should still check these out, which you can easily do online: Connectco (www. connectco.com), an accounting software program; and Apparel Associate Business software from Information Associates (www.as plus.com/products), which will not only help you figure out your finances but will also help you organize your inventory, accounts receivable and payable, sales and purchase order processing, and payroll functions. The same is true with AIMS (Apparel Information Management Software), which, in addition to accounting, will also help

Equipment and Fixtures Checklist

Use the following as a guide for outfitting your apparel store. It's been designed with the average 1,200- to 1,500-square-foot store in mind. Of course, if you've got something more expansive in mind, you'll have to make some modifications.

❑ Checkout counter $_____

❑ Cash registers   _____

❑ Mannequins   _____

❑ Tables   _____

❑ Hangers   _____

❑ Clothing racks   _____

❑ Lighting   _____

❑ Ticketing machines   _____

❑ Computer   _____

❑ Business/marketing software   _____

❑ Security alarms   _____

❑ Miscellaneous fixtures   _____

❑ Miscellaneous office supplies   _____

Total Store Equipment/Fixture Expenditures $_____

you integrate store functions like company setup, order processing, customer billing, shipping and invoicing, and accounts receivable.

Tight on Security

Not every "customer" who walks through your front door is going to want to pay for the merchandise he or she tries on. And unfortunately, we're not just talking about the obsessive browsers. We're talking about the inevitable shoplifters who at some point are going to force you to invest in some kind of security equipment, whether it's two-way convex mirrors, burglar alarms, or a closed-circuit television.

Again, a number of factors will determine how much you'll need to invest in security equipment, namely the size and location of your store. If you're a small-store owner in a small town, you probably won't have to invest in a $6,000 closed-circuit television. You might do just as well with two-way mirrors, tamper-proof price tags, security hangers, and the electronic tags and/or tickets we talked about that must be removed at the time of sale and that set off an electronic alarm if taken out of the store.

Some store owners shy away from any kind of security equipment, believing that it creates an unpleasant atmosphere and alienates customers, but we certainly wouldn't recommend leaving security up to chance. Also, if your store is in downtown Chicago, or in any high-crime metropolitan area, you'd be wise to think about some kind of high-security system. If you can afford it and will only sleep at night knowing you have an expensive closed-circuit TV in your store, by all means, go for it. Otherwise, our resident expert T.J. Reid says that many apparel store owners find that installing fake closed-circuit systems also deters shoplifting. Studies show that the effectiveness of a

> **Tip...**
>
> ## Smart Tip
>
> To eliminate shoplifting, keep your displays low, avoid hidden areas, and station one of your employees at a sales counter positioned near the door to observe customers as they leave.

Say No to Shoplifting

Train employees—your store's most important "fixture"—to become familiar with some of the telltale signs of a shoplifter. For one, shoplifters are often nervous; they spend more time looking around to see if anyone is watching than they do looking at merchandise. They also might hover around one specific area or carry merchandise from one department to another in hopes of confusing salesclerks. Shoplifters often carry shopping bags, briefcases, or backpacks, or wear heavy clothing—such as a baggy coat—out of season.

One of the best deterrents to shoplifting, especially if you're reluctant to use one of the monitor devices, is alert and attentive employees. Having your employees greet each customer with a cheerful "Can I help you?" will make customers happy and let potential shoplifters know that the salesperson is attentive to who is in the store. Also stress to your employees the importance of being familiar with the prices of your merchandise. An employee who knows that a pair of designer sunglasses should cost more than $5 will be able to prevent a thief from getting away with switching the price tags.

Finally, make sure there is a clear view from the cashier to the front door, have your fitting rooms regularly—and unobtrusively—patrolled by a clerk, and keep your expensive merchandise at the rear of the store.

closed-circuit TV system—real or fake—is heightened by posting signs in your store window announcing that you have it.

You'll Want to be Alarmed

Beware!

Apparel industry figures show that sales personnel steal twice as much merchandise as outside shoplifters. Check the references of all applicants and restrict access to any safes and keys to only your most trusted employees.

Even if you believe extensive security will hinder your store environment, you should read the following for future reference, especially if you plan a major store expansion:

- *Local alarms.* Local alarms are tamper-proof bells outside the building that aren't connected to an alarm company or police station. In theory, the noise of the alarm would frighten away a burglar, and neighbors would call the police. Often, however, these alarms are ineffective in out-of-the-way locations where police patrols are infrequent and there are no neighbors to hear the alarm.

- *Silent alarms.* Silent alarms will not sound on your store premises but are connected to either a police station or a security company station, which will notify police in the event of a break-in. Silent alarms are recommended as deterrents against both armed robbery and burglary, but many experts suggest they be backed up by a local alarm.

- *Perimeter or entry protection alarms.* Perimeter and entry protection alarms are placed at the building's various entry points. Burglars recognize the risk involved in trying to deactivate an entry alarm, which is their main deterrent value.

The Well-Dressed Office

In your back-office setup, you can trim costs by going with the minimum, such as a small desk, a chair, and one or two 29-inch locking file cabinets. You probably will also need bookshelves for the many catalogs, magazines, and pricing guides you'll be referring to in buying and appraising inventory. You can probably get by for less than $500 if you buy used furniture and shop around for it. In this space, you might also want to install a soft drink machine, a microwave, a refrigerator, and/or a coffee maker for your employees.

- *Space protection alarms.* These alarms monitor the interior spaces of the store through sound waves or passive infrared beams that detect movement or sounds.

Most stores require more than one kind of alarm system. For $500 to around $2,500 (depending on individual needs), you can have a combination of two or three different alarm systems installed in your store that warn of different types of illegal entry and ring in the store and/or at the alarm company's station when activated. Many experts also advise store owners to equip their alarm systems with a backup power source in the event of power failure.

Shopping center and mall tenants usually receive the services of a security patrol as part of their common area fees, but many store owners like the extra assurance of burglar alarm systems.

Getting the
Goods

Don't think that just because you're carrying some of the spiffiest millennium merchandise at the best prices your clothing is going to automatically fly off the shelves—or that it will even be in style six months from now, when you have more hoodies in stock than the local high school.

Our point? Capitalize on all of the market research you've done to make the most of your merchandising. Stay on top of fashion, but recognize the needs of your own customers vs. those on another coast. Be able to discern a classic from a fly-by-night trend. Know how much inventory to buy. Be prudent when necessary. Read on.

Tracking the Trends

The most common mistake made by apparel store owners is buying according to their own personal tastes. This doesn't mean that you should ignore your instincts, but you should look beyond your own closet.

Clothing marts, where clothing manufacturers always have their merchandise on display, are great places for apparel buyers and retailers to spot trends. If you're on or near the West Coast, the California Mart in Los Angeles serves the entire West Coast with more than 4,000 reps and 8,000 lines in its downtown location. Otherwise, look under "Clothing" in your local Yellow Pages for marts in your area.

Merchandise on display in marts usually leads the season by six months, with most new styles starting on the West Coast or in New York or Europe. When browsing, make sure you not only look at all the new lines but also take the time to meet clothing reps and ask plenty of questions regarding trends, fabrics, and prices.

Whatever you do, never depend on any one source for the definitive word on what's "in" this season. Always get second and third opinions from clothing reps, and while you're at it, try to corroborate their opinions with what you read in fashion magazines and the apparel trades.

It never hurts to cultivate a relationship with the editor of your favorite publication. They can often give you insight into some new style or trend materializing in one or more parts of the country.

Make-or-Break Buying

Smart buying and inventory control are essential to your store's bottom line, and because few independent store owners can afford to hire a designated buyer in the beginning, you may find yourself doing double or—dare we say—triple or quadruple duty as a buyer.

Normally, you'll want to make your purchases six months in advance and have the merchandise delivered three months before the season

Fun Fact

For the Christmas season (August buying season), you may do three times as much buying as any other time.

begins. For example, in January you'll purchase summer clothing; in April, fall fashions; in August, holiday wear; and in October, spring clothes. We'll tell you right now—there's more to buying that just being able to select the right merchandise. You've also got to know a thing or two about fabric, be a skilled negotiator (which we will go into later), and know where you can find an alternative supply of the same style if a specific manufacturer cannot give you a reorder in time for the season.

Some apparel retailers hire buyers on commission. If there's a small chain in your state (four or five stores) with a full-time buyer, visit some of the outlets and evaluate what you see. If the buyer appears to know what he or she is doing, approach the store manager and offer to pay an additional percentage if the buyer will make purchases for you when visiting the mart. Smaller chains often like this idea because you're helping absorb the cost of the buyer. For obvious reasons, you won't want the chain to have any of its stores in your immediate area. Not only will the buyer's loyalties not be with you; the chain will be selling the same items at a lower price.

If you're in the market for a local buyer, chat up your most trusted manufacturers' reps, who will be the most familiar with the competition and reliable buyers in your area.

Around the country, numerous apparel marts and merchandise marts with fashion showrooms allow authorized retailers and buyers for retailers to view apparel lines from manufacturers and wholesalers. The marts in large urban centers are usually

> ### ⚠ Beware!
> Suppliers often establish a minimum order for merchandise an apparel retailer wishes to purchase. They may also require that retailers also purchase a minimum number of items per order, which prohibits the store owner from purchasing only one or a few of a given item.

Exclusive Buying

While it is virtually impossible to secure exclusive rights to a manufacturer's goods, you can ask that a sales rep not sell identical merchandise to another store in the immediate vicinity. Some apparel store owners say that they prefer these local exclusives from their sales reps, such as Waynette Davenport-Ford of Davenport Designs in Savannah, Georgia, who features many distinctive products that can't be found elsewhere in the local area. The flip side to this position is that the supplier—assuming he or she agrees to give you the exclusive—might expect you to buy substantial amounts of his or her product to make up for lost sales to other stores in the territory.

Open to Buy Worksheet

With no past performance to provide guidance, the new apparel retailer must calculate the open to buy (OTB)—the dollar amount budgeted for inventory purchases for a given period (usually one, three, or four months)—in the same way initial inventory was calculated, which is by determining the amount of sales needed to pay store overhead and cover other costs.

But after the business has been operating from several months to a year, the store's inventory control system will indicate minimum inventory levels and monthly or seasonal sales volume. With this information, the store owner can determine the shop's OTB position using the following formula:

(Planned Inventory + Anticipated Sales) −
(Actual Inventory + Stock on Order) = Open to Buy

Most apparel retailers calculate their OTB seasonally to accommodate the variations in types of merchandise and sales fluctuations that accompany the seasonal nature of the apparel business. Use the worksheet below to track your inventory, sales, and budget.

Month	Planned Inventory	Anticipated Sales	Actual Inventory	Stock on Order	Open to Buy
January					
February					
March					
April					
May					
June					
July					
August					
September					
October					
November					
December					

both huge and permanent. See the Appendix at the end of this business guide for a list of the major U.S. marts.

Don't discount the value of cash in making a purchase. Small manufacturers are often cash-poor, and a buyer who shows up with money in hand can make a tremendous deal at times. Don't, however, buy just because you got a good deal. In this business, as is the case with any other, you really do get what you pay for.

Inventory Overload

In the apparel business, you can never be too lean. It's very easy to overbuy in this business and get stuck with duds that are, well, duds. The common mistake most apparel store owners/buyers make is buying too much of one thing, usually fad items that go out of style quickly (remember stirrup pants?). The general rule of thumb in the apparel business is to have wide enough inventory so that you're not always reordering, but not so large that you have a warehouse full of clothing you couldn't give away at a garage sale.

So what's the magic formula for a balanced inventory? Experienced apparel retailers recommend that a new store owner begin slowly with a relatively small inventory, which in the beginning may involve a lot of guesswork in picking and choosing until your customer base is firmly established.

Again, we're going to stress the niche idea again. "I knew that I wanted to differentiate myself in my market, so I went to New York and Los Angeles to learn how to buy," says Debbie Allen, whose store sells higher-end brands. "You also must invest in attending the major trade shows and be consistently focused, since styles change constantly. And be sure to attend every seminar you can to learn how to become more business savvy!"

As we've said, with men's clothing, there isn't so much of a guessing game. In fact, the biggest advantage you have with men's clothing is that men don't experience the same radical style shifts as women. Sure, there are fads that come and go, like the baggy linen suits that designers drag out every spring. But we will give the same advice as we did for the women's apparel. Even if you pride yourself on being the most cutting-edge clothier in your area, never

Beware!
When it comes to offering special deals and cash discounts, most clothing manufacturers tend to cater to chain stores that buy in mass quantities, not independent apparel store owners who buy their merchandise in a much smaller volume. So if the idea of buying bothers you, you might want to contact a company like D.L.S. Outfitters in New York City.

carry just what's trendy, or those baby blue drawstring pants will soon be on your 75-percent-off discount rack.

Mainstays like overalls and jumpers notwithstanding, today's children's clothes also experience style shifts, thanks to the popularity of stores like Baby Gap, Baby Benetton, and Old Navy. The same is true of the teen market, which readily follows what's being seen on fashion runways. How many times have you or a friend lamented, or bragged, that your kids were better dressed than you or your husband? For better or worse (we mean in your wallet),

this is all good news for the potential children's apparel store entrepreneur.

This may seem obvious—and keep in mind we're pretty much excluding the children's market here—but colors tend to be seasonal; in the winter, brighter colors move more slowly, so you'll be buying more black, brown, and gray. In the summer, obviously, the opposite will be true. (If you're opening a store in Palm Beach or Palm Springs, this tip doesn't apply to you.) One of the advantages that independent apparel stores have over chains is that department store lines and colors are usually limited. Yours don't have to be.

Make sure you or your designated buyer stay alert to sales as well as styles. Often at the end of a buying season, you can pick up a line that didn't sell well for a fraction of the cost. Why would you want to do this? Well, if you do happen to open a store in south Florida, where yellow Polo shirts sell well year-round, you might be able to get them cheap if there happened to be a surplus in the Northeast, where store owners obviously didn't read this business guide!

Don't Let Clothes Get Cold

As we illustrated by our seasonal buying example, most stores turn inventory between three and four times a year. Turning inventory four times a year means you should have a three-month supply on hand. If you expect $30,000 a month in sales, your stock should then amount to around $90,000. In general, the higher your store's turnover rate, the more inventory you'll require and the larger your initial investment will be.

To determine how much of each stock item is necessary to have in your store or on order, apparel retailers sometimes evaluate turnover rates for their merchandise against actual sales of that merchandise. For example—and this is not college calculus—say the turnover rate on dress shirts is 4.5 times per year. Divide 52 (weeks in a year) by 4.5 and you come up with 11.5 weeks—the amount of time it should take your inventory of dress shirts to turn over. To go a step further, if your sale of dress shirts averaged $250 per week during one complete turnover (11.5 weeks), then you know that you need to eventually buy about $2,875 worth of dress shirts (at retail value) when you next order from your suppliers.

> **Tip...**
>
> ## Smart Tip
>
> Skirt lengths generally move up and down faster than the stock market, so even if you pride yourself on being the hippest women's clothing store in town, never carry just what's trendy.

We realize this is an elementary illustration of how inventory planning is done. You will learn best how to plan your inventory from your own experience and by using consultants.

Tracking and Tagging Merchandise

We probably don't need to tell you that there's more to inventory control than simply buying new products. You need an adequate stock control system to tell you what merchandise is in the store, when it will arrive, what's been sold, and how to price all of the merchandise and accessories in your store.

Some apparel store owners find that tracking inventory via a manual tag system is effective because it just involves keeping track of all tags that are removed when an item is purchased. You can even use the tag system to maintain sales records and from those records produce a monthly chart representing sales according to product line, brand name, and style. Along the top of the chart, list your various product lines and down the left margin, list the various brand names and their different styles. At the intersecting spaces down the column you would mark how many of each brand name were sold, in what style and color and any other distinguishing features, whether they were on sale or discounted, and any other relevant information.

Stat Fact

It costs the average apparel retailer anywhere from 20 percent to 30 percent of his or her original investment in inventory just to maintain it. That means if you turn your inventory four times during your fiscal year, it will cost you from 5 percent to 7.5 percent of your sales just to maintain this inventory.

If your store is small enough, you can also use the oh-so-sophisticated method of simply eyeballing your shelves or, in conjunction with price tags, use bin tickets—tiny cards kept with each type of product that list a stock number, description, maximum and minimum quantities stocked, cost, selling price, and anything else of interest. Bin tickets, in addition to price tags, correspond to office file cards that list a stock number, selling price, cost, number of items in the store, supply source, order dates, quantities, and delivery times.

Believe it or not, the price tag's design can also help to streamline clerical functions. We suggest using two-part tags with a perforated separation with identical information on each half. When a sale is made, it's easy to remove half the price tag and set it aside. At the end of the day, you match up the numbers on the tags with your sales receipts.

While we're on the subject of price tag design, here's an idea: In the tags' "style" space, you might want to put a code number or letter that identifies clothing and accessory categories (A for dresses, B for blouses, C for belts, etc.). You can also use colored tags—say, different colors for each month. This will tell you how long an individual item has been on the selling floor. A color code system also makes it easy to go through inventory quickly and decide what items on the racks have to be cleared or reduced.

Except for a sticker that allows you to indicate a price change, don't put a new tag on any item once you've marked it. Otherwise, you defeat the purpose of having coded or specialized price tags.

Bring sales receipts into the equation, and you can use these and price tags as backup for each other. The price tags are an efficient record of the fact that a sale of a certain item has been made. The receipt is a convenient record of the fact that a sale has been made to a certain person.

Suitable Suppliers

Depending on your inventory selection, you may need just a few suppliers or dozens of them. Sometimes, suppliers will find you through sales reps who will come knocking on your doors. More often, particularly when you're starting out, you'll need to locate suppliers in any number of places: trade shows, the wholesale showrooms at clothing marts, conventions, in buyers' directories, through industry contacts, the Business-to-Business Yellow Pages, and trade journals. In general, suppliers are divided into three categories:

Tip...

> ## Smart Tip
> It's important for you to learn each of your suppliers' order-filling priorities. Some suppliers fill orders on a first-in, first-out basis; others give first attention to the large orders while customers with small orders wait. Consequently, most retailers specify a cancellation date on their orders. Goods shipped after this date are returned to the supplier.

1. *Manufacturers.* Most apparel retailers buy either through company sales reps or independent reps who handle the merchandise of several companies. Prices are usually lowest from these sources, unless your location makes the shipment more costly.

2. *Distributors.* Also known as wholesalers or jobbers, distributors use quantity discounts to buy from two or more manufacturers and then sell the goods to retailers. Although their prices to you are higher than a manufacturer's, they can also supply independent retailers with small orders from a variety of manufacturers. (Some manufacturers refuse to break case lots to fill small orders.) Also, the lower freight bill and quick delivery time from a nearby distributor will often compensate for the higher per-item cost.

3. *Import sources.* Many menswear retailers buy foreign-made clothing from a domestic import concern operating much like a domestic wholesaler. Many retailers also travel abroad at least once a year to buy and import merchandise.

Display Supplier Savviness

Reliable suppliers are an asset to your business, and you must treat them as such. While a certain amount of bargaining comes with the territory, and you want to look for the best deal possible, you can't ask suppliers to shave prices on everything, and you must pay your bills on time. Once you've developed a working relationship, you may be able to ask to have your billing cycle extended.

- *Obtaining credit.* Merchandise wholesalers tend to be cautious, and in the beginning you won't be able to provide trade references or a bank credit rating. So in this case, a personal financial statement and an honest demeanor count for a lot. Some suppliers will even agree to put you on a COD basis in the beginning and then issue you a line of credit later.

- *Discounts.* It makes sense to review the terms of purchase and never pass up discounts. The most common discount is given for prompt payment—for example

2 percent–10 days; "net 30" is often printed on invoices. This means that you can deduct 2 percent from the total invoice if you make a payment within 10 days and that the entire amount (with or without the discount) must be paid within 30 days. If you can pay immediately with cash, and if you already have an established working relationship, ask your suppliers if you can get an additional cash discount.

According to author T.J. Reid, the secret to requesting markdowns, sending back goods, paying bills late, and keeping any discount agreement you may have is in your attitude. Be professional and speak with knowledge and confidence. Don't whine and make excuses for making a late payment. This is the attitude that will serve as your money-back guarantee.

A Functional, Fashionable Facility

An apparel store can be opened in as little as 1,200 square feet, though a number of the apparel store owners in this business guide have interiors of 2,000 square feet or more. Typically, mall locations, which didn't apply to our entrepreneurs, offer more restricted areas, usually less than 1,000 square feet.

Storage/office space is an important part of the floor plan for an apparel store; it's often used to handle shipping and receiving and related chores, to take care of paper-

Gotcha!

Customers coming in your front door behave like pedestrians on the street. Those who know what they want head directly for it, while those who don't know (the "just looking" crowd) move from place to place as their interest is caught by goodies on display and/or sale items. These two types of customers are often referred to as "destination" and "shopping" traffic.

Destination customers move in planned, logical sequences. Shopping customers take a random approach, usually drifting to the right after they enter your front door. Destination traffic will generally turn left to avoid crowds. What does this mean? Put your store specialties, like Michael Starr T-shirts or multicolored surf shorts, directly to the left of the entrance, where destination customers will be able to complete their purchases quickly. Put higher-ticket and lower-replacement items, such as coats and suits, to the right to attract the attention of the shopping traffic.

work, and to store extra inventory. You should plan office/storage space to be in the range of 10 to 25 percent of your total floor area.

"Everything we see now is trendy and clean, with simple window displays, no matter what price level we're looking at," says Stillwater, Oklahoma, apparel entrepreneur K.C., "so the last thing you want to do is give the appearance of being outdated. Market perception is everything. In the restaurant business, atmosphere is often No. 1, and the quality of the food is No. 2. The same can be said in the apparel business; atmosphere is often No. 1, and the quality of the clothes is No. 2. Look at the popularity of stores like Old Navy."

"It doesn't matter what kind of merchandise you have unless it's well-organized," reiterates Dr. Nancy Stanforth, associate professor at Kent State University's School of Fashion. "These days everyone's competing with the Gap to have a clean, neat, and organized store. It is all about visual merchandising."

> ### Bright Idea
> Practically every major city hosts one or more trade shows relevant to the apparel business. Contact your local chamber of commerce and/or convention bureau for the shows in your city or state. The annually published *Tradeshow Week Data Book* lists important data on all trade shows in the United States. You can look for the book at the library, contact the publisher at Tradeshow Week at (323) 668-1450, or visit their web site at: www.tradeshow week.com.

And why not? The Gap's merchandising strategy has been one of the most successful in the apparel business. The store's clean, uncluttered look with polished wood floors and tables with neat stacks of tops in varying colors has become its much-copied hallmark.

Design your layout with these general objectives in mind: Exhibit merchandise within the store to take advantage of customers' natural traffic patterns and to encourage high traffic flow in certain areas of the store. Place lower-priced impulse merchandise, such as hair accessories and jewelry, in the front of your store. Put more destination merchandise, like suits and/or coats, at the rear or upstairs of your store. Expensive items should be highly visible but physically difficult to reach to minimize shoplifting and damage.

Wide-open aisles are best to allow customers a leisurely perusal, but also create the occasional "obstacle," such as a table with sale items customers can't help but notice.

Places, Everyone

We'll say it again: Simplicity sells. Your selling floor should be clean and uncluttered so that your merchandise stands out as the central focus. Hanging rods should be installed along the walls to display merchandise. An area with double rods can display blouses or jackets above and pants or skirts below. To accommodate the average customer height, rods should generally be fixed no higher than 5 feet, 6 inches and no lower than 3 feet, 6 inches. About 80 percent of the total selling floor should be devoted to hanging space and about 20 percent to shelving, depending on the merchandise. Free-standing clothing racks can be positioned around the rest of the selling floor, leaving enough room for customers to browse without bumping into each other.

> ## Bright Idea
> Aside from any eclectic furniture bargains you find, interesting music and plants can also add to the unique quality of your store.

"The typical men's store is a wall of sleeves," says Fred Derring, D.L.S. Outfitters president. "But what you want today is a store with no walls. On a subliminal level, people want to be told stories with clothes. They want to see a leather jacket with a pair of pants and a sweater, so they can tell you 'I want that outfit.' Everything's more touchy-feely these days. Customers want to touch fabric, look at belt loops, and really know what they're buying."

In keeping with our "simplicity sells" idea, the color scheme of your store should be low key (light, neutral colors) and, ideally, carry through to your store's signs, bags, and boxes. If you're going to open in a 1,200-square-foot facility, subdued colors make the store appear larger. Bright colors, on the other hand, tend to call attention to the surroundings rather than the clothes. According to our experts and entrepreneurs, wood floors are the perfect complement to a simple, airy design.

Display color-coordinated outfits inside the store. Many customers don't want to display their fashion failings and will often hesitate to ask a clerk whether a color matches or if a shirt matches a pair of pants. You can help in this area and increase sales by having color-coordinated displays throughout the store and doing things like showing two or three shirts with one particular pair of slacks.

Dressing Room Dos and Don'ts

Renowned writer and poet Maya Angelou once said, "I have lived in this body all my life and know it better than any fashion designer; I'm only willing to purchase the item which becomes me, and to wear that which enhances my image of myself to myself." That's where you and the dressing room come in.

Retail clothing owners are often so intent on fixing up the store front and displaying their wares that they forget about the dressing room. However, this is probably one of the most important sections of the store, as this is the place where most purchasing decisions are made.

Sample Layout of a 1,200-Square-Foot Facility

Within a rectangular space of 1,200 square feet, your clothing store should be able to provide for at least three dressing rooms, a carefully located checkout counter, an ample receiving-and-storage room, and lots of hanging and display areas.

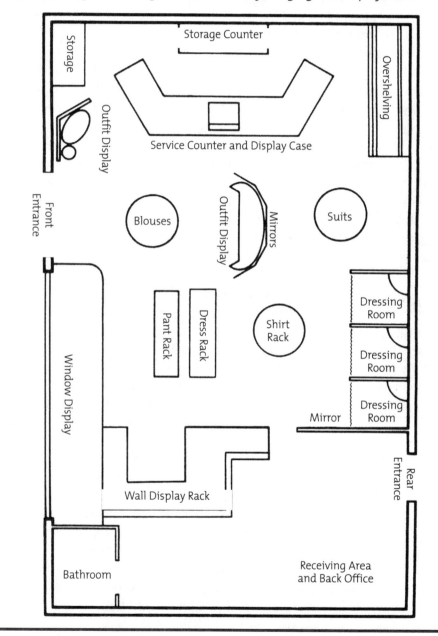

Unless your store is tiny (less than 1,200 square feet), the floor plan should include at least three dressing rooms. (Take our word for it: The only thing more frustrating for a woman than looking at herself in a dressing room mirror is not having enough room to try things on.) The simplest and least expensive way to construct dressing rooms is to build them against one wall, with wood partitions about 7 feet high. Hang a rod across the width of each room and put drapes on the rod.

Smart Tip

Allowing six or fewer items of clothing per customer inside the fitting room will help reduce theft.

Women's dressing rooms can be as small as 5 by 5 feet—no smaller than 5 by 7 feet for men—but the greater the square footage per room you allow, the more psychologically and physically comfortable your customers will feel trying on clothes.

After assuring your customers' comfort, make sure there is plenty of incandescent lighting and at least one mirror—two if possible. For a smaller store, an alternative is to have full-length mirrors outside the rooms. Paint the walls in a neutral, flattering shade that will help to reflect a healthy, glowing skin complexion in the mirror. Provide a bench or chair, a box of tissues, and have two or more hooks to hang clothes on. Also you or a sales associate should be available to bring the customers different sizes, make recommendations such as accessory items, and generally "ooh and aah" over their selections.

Window Displays

Passersby judge a store by what they see, and the first thing to catch their eye will be your store's window display. Trimming a window or display area with well-appointed mannequins might seem to be a purely decorative aid to make a store look enticing, but you heard D.L.S. Outfitters' Fred Derring. These days, your store should tell a story. Creative, storytelling displays put customers in a buying mood and sell merchandise.

Bright Idea

If window dressing puts you in a bad mood, you might want to check out the competition or the design department of a local college for ideas. If you can afford a little extra expense, you might want to put an ad in the paper for an interior design professional.

When appropriate, coordinate your window displays with any national advertising you may be doing. Most stores, for example, will either include pages from the publication along with a placard saying, for example, "As Advertised in GQ." Also, seasonal displays in conjunction with holidays can offer you opportunities for originality and related-item selling. They also help build your store's reputation for merchandising alertness.

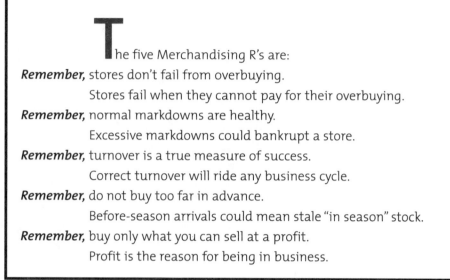

Counter Intelligence

In many stores, you find the checkout counter in the center of the store, surrounded on four sides by tables or some configuration, like mirrors. Directly across from the cash register, you'll also normally find the dressing rooms and/or mirrors, which is no accident. With your register and checkout counter centrally located, your sales clerks can watch all areas of the store. You can also see when a customer needs help and be on the lookout for suspicious shoppers. Aside from theft protection, if mirrors are near the checkout counter, the clerk can always offer helpful comments when the customer is trying on clothes. Another option is to have your checkout counter located near the front section of your store, where you can keep an eye on incoming and outgoing foot traffic. Whatever you decide to do, be sure you have a clear line of vision from checkout to front door.

If you want to provide your employees with a coffee or soft drink machine, make sure it isn't located near any merchandise. A small table with a couple of chairs and perhaps a small refrigerator will suffice for an employee lounge.

12

Sizing Up the
Market

Whether you decide to specialize in high-end fashion or sporty casual merchandise, never lose sight of what sets you apart from Target, Sears, and all the other apparel chain stores. You may not be able to mark down a pair of jeans to $9.99, but what you do have going for you is the old adage: "You get what you pay for."

▲

"Department stores all look alike because merchandisers like Ralph Lauren, Tommy Hilfiger, and Nautica are all fighting for the same brand space," says Fred Derring, principal of New York City-based D.L.S. Outfitters, which helps retailers market their stores. "If you moved the marquee, you wouldn't know whether you were in Bloomingdale's, Macy's, or Lord & Taylor. And when everything begins to look alike, consumers can become disenchanted. In addition, people just don't have as much time to shop today, and when they do, they want to go into a store and be serviced properly. Forget service with a smile. If you can even find someone to help you in most department stores, you're lucky. The rest of them seem to live by the rule that the less payroll, the better.

"Small stores are more focused on the community," Derring adds. "They know their customers better, they give terrific service and they generally have a more interesting collection of clothes on their store floors that will add to making customers feel special. These are the kinds of features customers are looking for in a smaller, independent store."

Differing Demographics

After that pep talk, you might just assume that reeling in customers will be a snap. Maybe, depending on your location. But don't let anything—even a killer location—prevent you from conducting more than a little market research so that you have a crystal clear idea of who your customers are. And as you'll see below, that research will vary somewhat, depending on the kind of store you plan to open.

If the idea of marketing or market research seems as remote a concept as programming your VCR or TiVo, we'll make it easy with our Marketing for Neophytes example. Let's go back to your inner child and pretend it's a hot summer afternoon that finds you and your friend Bill sweating it out under the shade of an elm tree in your front yard.

"Boy, it's hot," Bill says. "I sure could go for a glass of lemonade. But I don't feel like walking eight blocks to go to Hillary's lemonade stand."

And that's when the lightbulb goes on in both of your heads. With no lemonade stand for eight blocks, you and Bill have found an untapped market of thirsty customers. You start by asking the neighbors if they would buy lemonade from you and learn that the heat also makes them too lazy to move, and they, too, would welcome some fresh-squeezed lemonade right in their own backyard rather than having to walk all the way down to Hillary's lemonade stand. Voilà! You're in business, and you've just had your first experience conducting market research.

While comparing lemonade to clothing may seem like comparing lemons to mangos, the tenets of market research are the same in every business. You've got to find out what the market will bear—and in your case, what the market will wear.

In the apparel business, as in others, you want to learn all about the demographics and psychographics of your market. Demographics are statistics such as age, gender, income level, geographic location, occupation, and education level. Psychographics are lifestyle factors, including special-interest activities, philosophical beliefs, social factors, and cultural involvements. As you will find out in your own research, white-collar professionals and business executives and their families differ from blue-collar workers in their clothing purchasing interests and needs; a suburban clientele usually differs from one that comes from a densely populated urban center; families have different interests and needs than most thirtysomething singles.

> **Fun Fact**
>
> Social class, a function of income, occupation, education, culture, upbringing, and other factors, strongly influences customers' tastes and spending habits. Residents of a particular community or neighborhood may be of different social classes, but generally there is some class uniformity within communities.

Let's look at a practical example of apparel demographics and psychographics. Common sense would tell you that you might not want to open a store called Leisurewear for Liberals in Kennebunkport, Maine, where prominent Republicans, like former president George H.W. Bush and his family, have homes. Similarly, you wouldn't open a men's surf shop on the campus of Barnard College, an all-women's school in New York.

However, it would show good business sense to open a stylish yet affordable clothing store in the middle of a bustling college campus with yearlong foot traffic. "My family has been involved in running small-town department stores my entire life," says K. Cohlmia, whose clothing store is located close to the campus of Oklahoma State University in Stillwater, Oklahoma. "When I was in college, I started to work for a man here in town in the clothing business. I could see that Stillwater would be a good town in which to open an apparel store because there was room for growth. Back then, there weren't many big malls, and the campus was growing."

Determining growth potential is one of the major components of market research, which brings us back to demographics, psychographics, and clarifying your target market. Once you identify the characteristics your customers—whether we're talking about women, men, children, liberals or surfers—have in common, you can find out whether to plan to stay in town for a while.

Here's what we know about the three basic customer groups:

Women

Let's start with the hardest first. If you're going to open a women's apparel store, you already know that the tastes of the "fickle" female customer are hard to stereotype. Every expert we spoke with agreed that the very first thing a prospective women's apparel retailer must do is decide where the "market-vendor" gaps are. In other words, which customers in the store's trading area will you serve, and what apparel can you provide (and at what price) that can't be found easily elsewhere? Once this is determined, you can buy accordingly.

"'What do I have that will entice a woman into my store?' is the big question every women's apparel store owner needs to ask. Yes, we know that's easier said than done, and it really depends on where you're going to open your store. There's a huge difference in consumer mentality across the country, and a store owner in Duluth is going to have to plan differently than one in Los Angeles.

Still, in considering your own market and potential customers, you'll want to get a handle on how the average woman thinks about clothes, even if she doesn't necessarily act on those thoughts. One of the experts we talked to spells it out: "A bank teller in her twenties wants to wear short skirts and show off her cleavage. And most twentysomethings, with or without big careers, are bargain shoppers. In her early thirties, a woman who's single is likely to read *Marie Claire* and starve herself for a couple of months to buy that Prada or Kate Spade bag. She's a slave to fashion and the color black, and her credit cards are maxed out if she hasn't yet 'made it' in her career. Another typical boutique female customer, usually in her late thirties and forties, reads *Town and Country* magazine and favors Chanel suits. And except for Chanel suits, taupe is her color of choice for clothes." Granted, these are generalizations that certainly don't hold true for every woman in every city across the United States, but it certainly is fashion for thought.

> **Bright Idea**
> If you want to truly study a community's economic base before you make plans to move in, you can find all sorts of information at your local chamber of commerce or the U.S. Bureau of the Census, which publishes studies on the numbers of firms in different lines of business and the populations of the communities where they are located.

Men

The typical male customer is between 18 and 40 years of age, with a smaller percentage in their 50s. (We didn't even bother listing a female customer's age because, frankly, women of all ages like to shop.) The male consumer is often single and usually has money to spend—but typically still has to be brought in kicking and screaming by his girlfriend or wife to spend it on clothes. His job may not require a coat and tie, but unless he's working in Silicon Valley with hipster entrepreneurial types, he still wants to look good.

As we've said, if given the choice, most men would rather throw a bridal shower than shop for a new sport coat. The only good thing about the business casual movement is that because of the trend, men seem more willing to be dragged into a clothing store.

Survey Says . . .

If you're considering opening a store in your local mall, consider these recent statistics gathered by the International Council of Shopping Centers (ICSC):

Shopper Profile
- ○ The median age of mall shoppers is 39 years.
- ○ Shoppers aged 35–44 spent more money at mall shops than department stores. On the other hand, department stores sold more to shoppers aged 55–64.
- ○ The median household income of mall shoppers is $51,000. However, mall shoppers' incomes are significantly greater than the average U.S. household's.
- ○ Large malls (over 800,000 square feet) drew less purposeful shoppers (32 percent) than regional malls (400,000 to 800,000 square feet), who had 39 percent purposeful shoppers. Regional mall shoppers also spent $15 more per trip than shoppers at the large malls.
- ○ Shoppers are—no surprise here—predominantly female (64 percent) compared to men (36 percent).

Shopping/Purchasing Habits
- ○ Mall shoppers are less purpose-driven than they were in the 1990s. At least 44 percent come to browse compared to 34 percent ten years ago.
- ○ The number of stores entered per mall trip has risen slightly from years past, from 2.6 to 2.9 stores.
- ○ Shoppers make purchases at 56 percent of the stores they visit.

Children

Even though little girls have been known to throw temper tantrums when they're forced to wear gingham jumpers to preschool, we're not really targeting kids here. We're aiming more for their parents—at least the parents of children up to age 10; those who still make the executive decision when it comes to their clothes. Typically, you can categorize these parents as yuppies, white-collar urban professionals who usually have a dual, and disposable, income.

Obviously, the more financially stable parents are, the more they'll be willing to spend on boutique clothing for their children—if they're into clothes themselves, that is. Don't forget what the Santa Monica-based children's clothier said about the clientele in her wealthy neighborhood. Just because they've got money doesn't mean they're spending it on Christian Dior and Jessica McClintock for tots. They may well be shopping at Target and socking the rest away for a college education at an expensive Ivy League school. It all goes back to doing your homework. If you're in an old-money, Mercedes or Lexus SUV-driving, Top-Sider-wearing area, you can bet those parents may not necessarily be shopping at Target or Sears, but they may be shopping the Gap or Gymboree sales. If you're in a more flashy nouveau riche area where mothers are driving Jaguars and wearing diamond tennis bracelets, or even one where the women spend

Fun Fact

The bulk of children's clothing sales—up to 60 percent—comes from those cute matching outfits, like top-and-bottom coordinates. When it comes to colors, seasonal trends like animal prints come and go, but consistent top sellers are still—no surprise here—light blue, pink, and green.

$200 on their own designer jeans, that's a market for children's fashionable boutique clothing.

The other thing you have working in your favor as a children's clothing store owner is that, these days, parents are simply having fewer children. In part, this has to do with the fact that women are marrying and having children later, and it also has something to do with more population- and financially-sensitive parents. Couples now realize just how expensive children really are and as a result are more likely to have one or two children at most. But this can just as easily translate into one or two really well-dressed children, if you get our drift.

Detailed demographic information should be available from established sources and apparel industry trade associations, like those listed in this book's appendix. Whatever you use, look for the following: (1) purchasing power (degree of disposable income); (2) residences (rented or owned; houses, condos, or apartments); (3) places and kinds of work; (4) means of transportation; (5) age ranges; (6) family status; and (7) leisure activities.

Canvassing for Customers

It's a pretty safe bet that a Top-Sider-wearing mother whose kids are wearing bright green Polo shirts and webbed belts will not be shopping for your imported-from-India glitter-strewn apparel. Come to think of it, when it comes to kids' clothes, forget the glitter-strewn apparel altogether.

The easiest way to conduct a customer search is to simply increase your level of awareness, whether that means hanging out at the local mall or video store, volunteering at your local grammar school, or talking to other store owners. If this strikes you as an amorphous way of conducting something as serious as market research, here are some questions that will serve as a guide for your local sleuthing. You may want to carry this list around with you when you're at the video store or talking with others so you can jot down some notes.

- What is the age range and average age of your potential customers?
- What is the percentage of males?
- What is the percentage of females?
- What is the average educational level of your customers?
- Where do your customers live?
- What are the occupations of your customers?
- Where do your customers work?
- What is the average income level of your customers?
- What is the primary reason your customers shop at your store?

> **Bright Idea**
>
> If you really want to know your market, attend the biannual MAGIC show. MAGIC International is the world's largest and most widely recognized producer of trade shows for the apparel industry and currently produces shows for the men's apparel market (MAGIC); the women's apparel market (WWDMAGIC); and the children's apparel market (MAGIC Kids). MAGIC shows take place every February and August in Las Vegas. For more information, visit www.magiconline.com.

This is not rocket science. If you're living on the West Side of Los Angeles or in the South Beach area of Miami and you can drive ten miles in every direction without seeing a domestic car, well, bingo, you can bet money in Vegas that your customers are above average in education and income—and maybe debt level—and that their occupations are white-collar (or trust fund).

Similarly, if you're opening a store in a college town like Stillwater, Oklahoma, you can bet undergraduate tuition that your average consumer will not be driving a fancy car or have a lot of disposable income. Debt, yes. Lots of money to shop, no.

Pound the Pavement

We might refer you to someone like Fred Derring, whose New York City-based marketing and consulting company, D.L.S. Outfitters, among other things, "interprets" the market for clients like you, the independent apparel store owner.

"We feel the pulse of the market," says Derring. "This includes the general direction of consumer preferences and of things like marketing, advertising, promotions,

▲

⚠ Beware!

Telemarketing can be successful, but only if you have a good, well-targeted prospect list from a reputable company. Also make sure that you follow any "do-not-call" guidelines that your state may impose.

and store fixturing. We visit all the annual apparel trade shows and keep an eye on fashion trends in magazines, on TV, in movie theaters, and by daily people-watching. We share this information with our clients, who we try to meet up with at least six times a year at these shows.

"One of the things that we try to emphasize with all our clients is that consumers are constantly bombarded with so much stuff that they really need to find a way to stand out," says Derring. "We always tell them that the best marketing channel is some kind of direct mail piece that's targeted toward a specific customer. You can get a targeted mailing list with zip codes and income levels, and you know that your potential customer will receive it."

For all you marketing pacifists out there who have little desire to pound the pavement and prefer the prime-time mode of marketing research, or if you simply want to substantiate the research you've already conducted, we have a few other things to share with you:

CENSUS TRACTS

Almost every county government publishes population density and distribution figures that show the number of people living in specific areas and indicate population trends, such as the number of college graduates high-tailing out of town for better jobs. However, even you pacifists might want to make sure your desired neighborhood hasn't been infiltrated by shopping malls and mini-malls, and that the population hasn't aged so much that it makes no sense to open a children's apparel store.

MAPS

Maps that show the hub of your community's business and reflect the residents' major spending habits are usually available from your local chamber of commerce. As long as you're scouting store locations, you might also check out road maps that will help you determine how accessible or freeway-close your store site is to the general public.

MEDIA SOURCES

The sales departments of any local newspapers and magazines can provide you with business profiles. This will both help you check

Tip...

Smart Tip

We mean business about mixers. If you're not already a member of your local chamber of commerce, put that on your "to do" list today. It's one of the cheapest—and most fun—ways to check out your potential customers.

Market Research Checklist

Marketing Your Merchandise

Choose three unique angles that describe your store's niche:

1. _____

2. _____

3. _____

Clients for Your Clothing

Clarify the group(s) that would be interested in your clothing:

- ❑ Friends _____
- ❑ SUV-driving moms _____
- ❑ Teenage girls _____
- ❑ Yuppie men _____
- ❑ Blue-haired matrons _____
- ❑ Surf dudes _____
- ❑ Silicon Valley geeks _____
- ❑ Other _____

Your Competitive Edge

One or more of the following should be on your list:

- ❑ Safe, well-lit parking
- ❑ Evening hours
- ❑ Spacious in-store layout
- ❑ Superior customer service
- ❑ Special ordering
- ❑ Other _____

Double-Checking Demographics

Find out everything you can about the neighborhood and town in which you wish to open your store.

- ❑ Get on the internet.
- ❑ Read local papers.
- ❑ Talk to your peers.
- ❑ Watch the local news.
- ❑ Check with the human resources departments of large local employers.

out your apparel adversaries and the financial situation of your potential customers—if you can't already tell by the number of foreign cars on your city streets. Your local Yellow Pages will also help you gauge the competition.

COMMUNITY ORGANIZATIONS

Most local chambers of commerce hold monthly mixers that are great schmooze fests for the new business owner on the block. This is a great time to get to know your competition and also spread the word about your store's grand opening or year-end sale.

Fun Fact

Old Navy—with its canine mascot, Magic, chosen because he looked like "Every-man's dog"— has gone into unique marketing arenas, such as sponsorship of an Indy 500 racing team.

Hold the Blue Light Specials

Whether we're talking women's, men's, or children's apparel, specialization will be key to your marketing success in this business. What better way to set yourself apart from your competitors than by having something different—and not just more expensive—to offer than the store down the street. You might laugh at our Leisurewear for Liberals example, but it's a creative marketing tactic nonetheless and could be successful in the right—no pun intended—market.

Let's review the marketing tactics of our own entrepreneurs for a minute. Waynette Davenport-Ford's Savannah, Georgia, specialty store caters to tourists and locals alike by selling merchandise that is hard to be found anywhere else locally. The Wooden Nickel in Stillwater, Oklahoma, caters to a college clientele with casual yet brand-name awareness. In Scottsdale, Arizona, Debbie Allen found a designer niche for sophisticated urban women with money who live and vacation in the area. Marcia Sauters, who owns the children's store in Santa Monica, carries personalized specialty items to make her stand out from the other children's apparel stores in the area.

In short, you can call this honing of your store's marketing SWOT. "Over the years, one of the things I've always conducted with my marketing department is SWOT," Cohlmia says. "SWOT stands for Strengths, Weaknesses, Opportunities, and Threads and is really just about doing a little self-analysis with regard to where the store and our clothes stand in the marketplace. As I've evolved to having a store with more of a younger image, SWOT has helped me choose new clothing brands and also helped shape the change of other external things, like our store's sign."

The Competitive Edge

Go into the Gap, Sears, and even Target and then visit the other independent clothiers near you. Check out things like store layout, accessories, store hours, merchandise labeling, etc. Casually ask what's selling and subtly check out the price tags (at this point you may want to keep the list hidden). Also discreetly ask the store owner questions like "What seems to sell well?" "Who are your customers?" "Do you have a lot of repeat business?"

If you're really lucky, you may not even be able to visit any or most of the above because they simply don't exist en masse in your area.

Get to know your competitors at local chamber mixers. As we said before, have a "spy" infiltrate the local enemy lines to find out how your merchandise stacks up. You might even want to keep another one of our famous lists handy that details the following: you and your competitors' similarities; your own competitive niche, which, by the way, you should be able to rattle off at the drop of a hat by now; what makes your merchandise, or your competitors', more saleable; whether or not your competitors' businesses are growing; and a clear understanding of your competitive advantages and disadvantages.

OK, you've got your work cut out for you. Ready, set, SWOT!

Attention, All Shoppers

Pat yourselves on your well-clothed backs. You've targeted the local clothes-horses, stocked up on the latest fashions, and installed fancy new fixtures. Now all you need to do is generate a little well-heeled foot traffic.

Obviously, your store's advertising and promotional campaigns will be key in generating interest among potential customers. In this chapter, we'll talk about avenues that are clothes-specific, like the importance of a good direct-mail piece, as well as the coordinated use of other media, including television, radio, and print advertising.

An Important Accessory

There are lots of reasons why advertising is important for a business start-up, but in the apparel business it comes down to a couple of things: Not only do you want to convince potential customers once and for all that you've got more to offer than Banana Republic or Ann Taylor, you want to make sure you have a strong image, like Banana Republic or Ann Taylor. In short, you need to create the desire to come into your store instead of those of your more established apparel competitors. If your ideal customer never strolls past your store, you'll hope that he or she at least pays attention to the mail and mass media. In the apparel business, advertising can help make up for a less-than-ideal location.

Try to look at advertising not just as another business expense but as a way of building your sales. Whatever media you decide will work best within your community—and we'll offer plenty of options—your advertising campaign should be well-planned, distinctive, and consistent with your store image. Advertising informs your customers about the merchandise you carry and your store's special events, services, and sales. And it's also going to be all those things that Advertising 101 says it should be: simple, straightforward, informative, and eye-catching.

You'll have to decide the most effective way to advertise your store by taking a good look at your business and potential customers. In doing so, you might ponder the following questions that we asked in Chapter 12:

- How is my store different from my competition? (e.g., he sells Levi's; I sell dress pants)
- What quality merchandise do I sell? (e.g., he sells Levi's; I sell dress pants)
- What kind of store image do I want to advertise? (e.g., trendy, tailored, casual, chic)
- What customer services do I offer? (e.g., special-order clothing, free on-site tailoring, a children's corner)
- Who are my customers? (e.g., Beverly Hills matrons, Manhattan models)
- What are their tastes? (e.g., trendy, tailored, casual, chic)
- Why do they buy from me? (e.g., convenience, the only store in town that sells plus-size business suits)

Selling Clothes with Attitude

In the big apparel picture, touchy-feely is as important in advertising as it is in merchandising. "Not only is advertising essential in the clothing business," says Fred Derring, owner and president of D.L.S. Outfitters, "but it's also essential to sell attitude and lifestyle as much as the clothes themselves. Just look at the Tommy Hilfiger ads."

In the smaller, independent store owner picture, we'd recommend something a bit less controversial than Tommy Hilfiger or Benetton, yet a bit more sophisticated than "Come on down" to sell both clothes and a lifestyle. Remember, you want to create a good business image as well as increase your sales.

In fact, for the small independent store owner, we recommend creating a sense of immediacy. In this business, that means talk about a sale and the fact that you carry Karl Lagerfeld jeans. However, you are not Karl Lagerfeld, Tommy Hilfiger, or Benetton; this is not the time to show how erudite you are with obscure ads or to create the next Apple 1984 campaign. We're not kidding here. If Fiona's Fashions down the street is constantly busy and frequented by people with money, borrow what it's doing. After all, imitation is the most sincere form of flattery.

> ## Fun Fact
>
> In 1998, Tommy Hilfiger claimed its provocative ad campaign featuring a picture of a model sitting at a desk in a replicated Oval Office was not intended to be a political statement. The company agreed to withdraw the campaign after being contacted by the White House legal office for violating a long-standing policy against using the White House for advertising purposes.

Advertising and Public Relations

Now that you've formed a clear picture of your store in relation to your friend Fiona's, you'll want to take into consideration the many options available to you, including direct mail (very popular), business directories and resource guides, newspapers, radio, and TV (local cable is a winner among entrepreneurs).

A Direct Hit

Although direct mail is expensive for the number of people it reaches, it can reach a highly targeted audience. Direct-mail pieces are also likely to be noticed and kept—particularly if you're on someone's favorite store list and you're advertising an upcoming sale with a coupon or some other in-store special event. Many entrepreneurs interviewed for this business guide find that direct mail, whether it's a catalog, letter, flier, or coupon, is an efficient way of targeting customers. Robert Loeb says that 70 percent of Loeb's marketing strategy involves direct mailing.

U.S. postal laws provide special rates for odd-sized direct-mail pieces; check with your local post office. Just be aware that while bulk mail is relatively cheap, it can be both slow and perceived by the receiver as junk. First-class mail will leave a more favorable impression.

Mailing lists can be purchased from list brokers, which you can find in your Yellow Pages under "Advertising—Direct Mail." These lists come in just about every category, and since you've done your marketing homework, you already know the lists you want. The one-time rental fee for these names is between $35 and $50 per thousand, with a minimum rental of 5,000 names.

K. Cohlmia, owner of the Stillwater, Oklahoma store, says, "Most of our advertising is in the form of direct-mail postcards that we send out to a mailing list of between 3,000 and 4,000 people."

You can get more bang for your buck—or, to borrow those corporate buzzwords, "add value" to your direct mailer—by presenting some sort of bonus offer. Put something in the ad that will entice customers into your store such as a 20 percent off sale or a $5 or $10 coupon for purchase of something in your store. This can be an excellent way to generate business.

Once your store is established and you have a mailing list of regular customers, you can send out "goodwill" direct-mail pieces, like Debbie Allen in Scottsdale, Arizona, does. "If a customer's birthday is coming up," she notes, "we'll send them a card with a discount coupon inside."

Make Contact with Coupons

If you're not feeling altogether flush, a viable direct-mail alternative is a coupon mailer that groups retail businesses within a community together in a bound coupon book usually including advertisements, discounts, or special offers. The books are mailed nonselectively to all homes within a specific zip code, so they aren't as targeted as a direct-mail piece that you'd design yourself, but they can still have great pull. As a store owner, you pay a fee to the company producing and distributing the coupon books; these companies should be listed in your Yellow Pages.

Radio

Radio can be effective in your store's advertising mix if you're advertising not your store image but something concrete, like a year-end or holiday sale or a special store event, and if you're advertising locally, where you know potential customers are listening to your chosen station.

Advertising on small stations that broadcast to local markets have nominal fees, whether it's read by the announcer or taped in advance. These stations, most with power of less than 1,000 watts, only reach very small geographic areas, and their programs are specifically designed to appeal to the people in this limited market. When you buy time on a small station, you're not paying for wasted circulation, and you may even get the local DJ to come in and broadcast live from your store.

Television

If you're just starting out, you're probably not going to be buying time during "Desperate Housewives" or "Monday Night Football." You might, however, do like Meridian, Mississippi, apparel store owner Robert Loeb did and consider buying time on one of your local cable channels. Rates are usually pretty reasonable, and you can create your own interesting, affordable ad.

"If we are going for store image, we will always do television," says Loeb, "because it's very personal and you can be yourself, and you have the advantage of being able to show the inside of your store."

Newspapers

Newspaper ads are often used by suburban and small-town store owners, although Cohlmia points out, "not with the same consistency as direct mail."

More often, apparel store owners use newspapers as a way of advertising a big store promotion. "If we're having a clearance sale, we'll always go with newspapers," says Loeb.

Prices vary depending on the newspaper's circulation and the size of your ad. If your store draws its customers primarily from the local community, you might find newspaper advertising valuable at times other than when you're having a special sale, especially if you take advantage of special editions such as shoppers' guides.

Billboards

No, we're not nuts, and we know that billboards might never be included in your ad budget. Nonetheless, our experts insisted that we mention them, and someday you just may be able to afford to see your store's name in lights. As D.L.S. Outfitters' Fred Derring points out, "Billboards are terrific because they are almost like a direct-mail piece. You have a guaranteed audience, and there's plenty of repetition."

Magazines/Newsletters

In general, newsletters are great print vehicles for reaching specialized markets because circulations are typically small and targeted, and ad rates are reasonable. In the apparel world, however, you probably won't find an industry newsletter that will be simultaneously read by your customers and people—meaning insiders—like you.

Magazines, however, are a different story. National advertising rates may make *Glamour* or *Elle* prohibitive to the independent store owner. But if your store goes national, you'll want to look into magazines as an advertising avenue.

In the interim, we'd suggest advertising in your town's local weekly entertainment/lifestyle publications, which are generally distributed to local restaurants and/or hotels that may very well cater to your clientele. Promote a specific product or sale. Include a coupon as part of your display ad. Add an incentive such as a discount if a customer mentions the advertisement.

Yellow Pages

Using directory advertising, such as the Yellow Pages of the local phone book, is a very important marketing tool that is often overlooked. Believe it or not, people actually use these tomes for more than doorstops and birdcage liners. When a prospective customer is looking for specific products or services in the directory, they are an excellent prospect because they are actively looking for a store such as a bridal shop or children's boutique.

Placing your listing under the right category will be critical so people can find you. And you

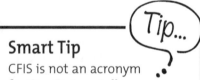

Smart Tip

CFIS is not an acronym for Can Fortunetellers Influence Sales? It's short for cost, frequency, impact, and selectivity, a broad advertising/marketing term that a newspaper or radio rep may throw around when talking about how much your ad will cost.

will increase the chances of a potential client seeing your business if you insert your listing under multiple headings or categories.

Business Cards

There's no news like good news in the clothes business, where the buzz of satisfied customers can mean nothing but more profit for you. As small as they are, business cards are a powerful marketing tool. Hand out these little gems at every opportunity. Think of them as mini-billboards that tell people who you are, what you do, and how to reach you.

A quick-print shop can do a nice, affordable job on your business cards by providing a variety of templates to choose from. You can also order them online from companies like Vista Print (www.vistaprint.com) for a nominal charge.

E-Commerce

A few years ago, only major corporations had web sites; today, an internet presence is as essential as a telephone and fax machine. A web site is your online brochure, and it can be working for you 24 hours a day, seven days a week.

You can expand your site by setting up a virtual store that is a lot like publishing a full color catalog, only better—and less expensive. Being only a click away is a tremendous convenience to customers who may only have time to shop during the wee hours of the morning.

Waynette Davenport-Ford, owner of Davenport Designs in Savannah, Georgia, says, "A lot of business owners focus only on their stores, but you really need to have other venues like a web site or an eBay store." Because Davenport-Ford operates her business in a seasonal location, certain times of the year are quite slow. "This winter has been really quiet," she says. "Thank God for my online sales through eBay and my web site. They really help to keep the store's merchandise moving out the door."

In her book, *Online Shopper's Survival Guide* (Entrepreneur Press, 2006), author Jacquelyn Lynn discusses the many benefits of shopping online, including the privacy of shopping in

> **Fun Fact**
> Levi's launched its first online sales effort in November 1998, showcasing more items than many department stores regularly stock. The site (www.levi.com) continues to offer consumers all sizes made in each line and displays its full line of clothing beyond jeans, such as shoes, belts, tops, skirts, and snowboarding jackets. The Levi's site is backed by newspaper and radio advertising, primarily in top college markets.

Reap the Rewards

In addition to signing up to be on the Wooden Nickel's mailing list, customers can also participate in their Royalty Rewards Program which has all kinds of in-store perks and benefits—and no strings attached. Regular customers simply fill out a form and are given a plastic card that is swiped each time they make a store purchase. For each $300 spent storewide, patrons are sent a $20 gift certificate. "With this system we're able to keep track of when the certificate is used and by whom," Cohlmia says. Gift certificates are also sent out when the customers initially sign up and when they celebrate a birthday to encourage repeat business. Cohlmia also says, "One of the neat things about this program is if someone hasn't been in for 90 days or more, we'll get a report and send them a little card with a gift certificate in that too."

your own home, taking time to research the product and make price comparisons, and not having to fight for a parking place or drive in inclement weather. "An estimated two-thirds of American households have at least one computer, and most of those systems have internet access," she says. "As the availability of high-speed internet access continues to rise and the cost continues to fall, people are spending more time—and money—online. It's estimated that by the year 2010, Americans will spend approximately $350 billion online."

Lynn also reminds us that Americans have been purchasing mail-order goods since Colonial times, when "ordering from a distance was a key element of American and even worldwide commerce." And when you do have a web site you are expanding your customer base by global proportions.

Don't Let Your Budget Burst at the Seams

How much is enough for an ad budget? That will largely depend on how big your store is and where it's located. Most businesses peg their ad budgets at 2 percent to 5 percent of their projected annual gross sales, generally referred to as the cost method, or, in this business guide, the commonsense method.

However, a realistic first-year advertising budget is at least 10 percent of projected gross sales, due to grand-opening campaigns and a bigger-than-normal initial advertising blitz. As you'll see when you read on, customers may not realize your store exists until they get your direct-mail piece, see that newspaper ad or billboard, or attend your grand-opening soiree. That's why advertising expenses are higher during the first few years.

Advertising has a cumulative effect, which means that responses may be slow at first but will increase with consistent hits. Sporadic splurges rarely pay off, and it's generally much better to advertise regularly on a small scale than to bust your budget on a Super Bowl spot.

A Grand Opening

Some apparel stores have done well with a big opening ad campaign, then coasted on a large amount of word-of-mouth advertising. However, the opening phase of your ad campaign will be the key to your long-term success. You should plan some kind of grand opening, preceded by a promotional campaign of some sort, like a direct-mail piece, newspaper ad, or Goodyear blimp (well, maybe).

Open your doors a few weeks before your grand opening. Your sign should be up and most or all of your inventory in the store. That way, when customers wander in to sample the punch and cookies, they'll also be enticed to sample your merchandise and friendly clothes-side manner. This is where great rumors will start about your store.

Besides punch and cookies, use whatever trick you can to hook customers into coming to your grand opening. Put up colorful flags or streamers to attract attention, stage a drawing for a small door prize, like some hip accessory, or give a small token to the first 50 people who purchase merchandise. Manufacturers' sales reps sometimes contribute promotional items if you tell them ahead of time about your grand opening. Also keep promotional fliers (with first-purchase discount coupons), business cards, gift certificates, and specialty advertising items in the store.

When you open your store, take a photo of yourself—in one of your store's outfits, of

▲

course—your staff or partners, and the building. Have the photo enlarged to an 8-by-10-inch glossy black-and-white print and then, to accompany the photo, write a brief history—we mean brief, not a white paper here—of your business, your background, your prospective customers and the need for your apparel store.

Send this press release to the city editor, or preferably to any editor with whom you have contact, of your local newspaper with the heading "For Release on XX Date." If you are running a grand-opening ad, send or hand deliver the release to one of the paper's ad salespeople (we'll warn you right now; you probably won't get past reception at The New York Times or

> **Beware!**
> If you locate in a shopping center or mall that is supported by huge ad budgets and the presence of large, popular chain and department stores, you will most likely generate revenue with little or no individual advertising. Of course, keep in mind that your rental expenses will be proportionately higher than those for an independent location.

any other metropolitan newspaper). Again, if you're able, and if you live in a small enough town, you can follow much the same process with your local TV and radio stations. In big metropolitan areas, TV and radio stations are less apt to read news off a press release, but, hey, if you're living in Stillwater, Oklahoma, where the radio and TV station personnel make house calls and stations sometimes have a slow news day, you may find yourself getting some free publicity.

Joining Forces

In the apparel business, the cost of advertising can be cut substantially by using co-op advertising, whereby clothing manufacturers agree to pay a portion of ad costs—including production and creative expenses—and will supply you, the apparel store owner, material to include in either a print, radio, or TV ad. Often, even the smallest of apparel retailers can get up to one-half of their ad costs reimbursed.

The major drawback to co-op advertising is that some manufacturers are more restrictive than others, meaning that they may set the rules governing how much of their product appears in and dominates the ad. You should also know that each vendor has a list of regulations for its co-op offers. Usually, as the store owner, you'll be required to send it details of what you did, such as a sale ad for jeans, and enclose the actual tearsheet, videotape, or audiotape, and the total bill from the newspaper, radio, or TV station.

Your Ad Dollars at Work

You should never stop surveying and studying your customers. Why? Because your community and customers' habits will change. If a customer drifts away, try to determine why. Yes, if you are on a first-name basis with your customers, like Cohlmia, Loeb, and most of the entrepreneurs interviewed for this guide, you have our permission to make that call directly. To make sure your ad dollars are being spent wisely, you might do the following:

- Advertise one item in one ad only, but make no references to the item in your window displays or anywhere inside the store. Simply count the calls and requests for the item.

- Run the same ad as a coupon to receive a special price or discount in two different publications with an identifying mark— like a check or asterisk—on each. See how many coupons come in from each source.

- Don't send out a direct-mail piece during a regularly scheduled sale and see if there is any change in your sales.

Dollar Stretcher

Handbills, printed on cheaper paper than direct-mail pieces and passed out on your street and in front of your store by your friendly sales staff, can be an inexpensive and effective way to announce your grand opening.

Make Progress with Promotion

In addition to consistent advertising, you'll need to do a certain amount of sales promotion to reward current customers and attract new ones, and to keep your name in the fashion-conscious public's mind. Apparel store owners often run promotions in the form of creative public relations activities, or special "sales" or contests.

Debbie Allen is the Promotion Princess of Scottsdale, Arizona. In the past, she has run an event she calls the "Shanghai Surprise." For the promotion, she sent out Asian-style pouches to customers on her store mailing list. In the bags were fortune cookies that, when broken open, told customers whether or not they were eligible for a store discount. Allen has also hosted in-store VIP parties, inviting customers to silent auctions that benefit organizations like the National Heart Association, and in the process, allowed customers and potential customers to see her store's wares. For many of Allen's in-store events over the years, manufacturers and sales reps have donated door prizes, which offers a double whammy of publicity for both the store owner and manufacturer.

Over the years, Allen has also sent her best customers $20 gift certificates on their birthdays. This kind of goodwill is excellent for word-of-mouth.

Offering to put on fashion shows for local women's groups can also be a smart promotional tack. Use the groups' own members for models, and you're almost sure to sell at least the garments they choose to wear!

In less glamorous terms, some of your promotions may simply depend on items you really want to get movin'. In this case, sidewalk sales attract a lot of attention and provide a good outlet for this kind of merchandise. Another promotional gimmick is to offer your merchandise

Tip...

Smart Tip

Grand openings aside, the most successful apparel retailers are personally well-known and liked in their communities. You, too, will need to become active in your community by joining and leading civic organizations, attending charity events, speaking at seminars, getting involved in politics, and attending openings of other businesses and events at local institutions.

Keep a Running Tab

Like author T.J. Reid, show your customers you care—and promote your store at the same time—with customer cards like the one below. Have customers fill them out when they make a purchase so you can mail them a discount gift certificate on a special occasion. For example, you can make the following cards: "Just Arrived," "Happy Birthday," "Shopping Invitation," and "Special Sale."

Name _____

Address _____

Phone _____   Birthday _____

Work phone _____   OK to call? _____

Spouse's name _____

Favorite labels _____

Pant/skirt size   _____   Sweater size   _____

Dress/suit/jacket size _____   Shoe size   _____

Blouse/shirt size   _____

at one set price for a limited time, the idea being to entice people into your store to browse through your merchandise.

Take it from apparel entrepreneur Allen and others: Plan your sales promotion activities at the beginning of each business year. You cannot host big events that might require the cooperation and participation of manufacturers and sales reps at the last minute. It's also smart to send press releases to the local media when staging a promotion; Allen has received a lot of local press that way.

Getting Prime Publicity

Local papers are most interested in local news, and that can very well include your store's silent auction. When you start your apparel store, when you have a sales promotion like a silent auction or fashion show, when you form a charitable alliance with a group like the National Heart Association, or when something of interest happens to you or your business, these are newsworthy events and worth letting the local media know about.

Why is publicity so important, and what will it do that advertising won't? Good publicity, like a successful promotional event, helps keep your store at the top of people's minds. Then there's the all-important factor of "reach" that ad professionals like to talk about. All reach means is that, with the right press release, you can place stories in more periodicals than you could afford to reach through paid advertising. Think about it; an article in a respected newspaper or magazine or an appearance on radio or television occurs only if it meets the standards of the editor or program director, which gives third-party credibility to your story—and your store—that cannot be duplicated with paid ads.

> ## Bright Idea
>
> Be sure to maintain a customer mailing list and send out cards announcing your specials. You might want to follow Scottsdale, Arizona, entrepreneur Debbie Allen's lead here and keep a guest book at the checkout counter, where customers can sign in after they make a purchase. It's another subtle way of letting them know you appreciate their business.

What's Your Sign?

Your sign is the most important contact between your apparel store and much of the outside world because it's usually the first thing a potential customer sees. Drive around town and observe which store signs catch your eye and, more important, which signs seem to have the most people walking underneath them through the store's front door!

Smart Tip

Tip...

Crucial to the design of your sign is a distinctive logo that can be printed on shopping bags and fliers.

"These days, you've got to have all the gimmicks, and that includes the right sign, especially if you are trying to change your image," says Stillwater, Oklahoma, apparel entrepreneur K. Cohlmia "Because we have been evolving and we are trying to attract the younger customers, changing our sign is literally an outward sign to the public that we've changed our image."

We've given you lots of advertising choices in this chapter, but it's up to you to decide just what combination works best for your apparel store. Like putting together that well-coordinated outfit, it's a process that may take time and some tweaking. But when you find that perfect fit, we guarantee that your store will turn heads!

14

For the
Record

We're just going to come right out and say it: If numbers make you nauseous, you may want to rethink a career in the clothing business. Pricing alone will give you heartburn. Then again, you may just need to find a good accountant or financial planner to help get you through the rough spots.

What we're really talking about here is an amplified version of what you do at home every month: Pay your bills and attempt to balance your checkbook. You may think the mere fact that your clothes don't stay on the shelves long enough to gather dust means your store is operating in the black. That may be, but we think a more exact profit measurement is important. Besides, information about your business's financial condition will help you identify and correct any income or expense problems before they make a huge dent in your store's profits.

With that in mind, we will discuss one relevant financial report in this chapter: the income statement. We will also discuss less calculating issues like the three C's of customer payment, tax deductions, and record-keeping.

Since most store owners will be starting out as relatively small independents, we're not going to provide you with the Banana Republic version of apparel financial statements.

The Income Statement: Short and Chic

An income statement, or profit and loss statement, charts the collections and operating costs of your business over a period of time, usually a month. In the beginning, if you're hoping to woo lenders, you'll want to create a projected income statement, which basically means you'll be making responsible and reasonable calculations about what your store profits will be for at least a year.

An easy way to estimate basic monthly sales and profits for your store is to first estimate the total seasonal buying patterns for your store, attributing varying percentages of the total volume to each month of the year. Yes, that was accountant speak, and you may want to let your accountant do the math. However, practically speaking, after all our discussions about buying, you should have a pretty clear idea of those patterns: a large—maybe even largest—volume of sales in late summer for preschool shoppers, a large volume of sales in the gift-buying holiday season between November and December, and a relatively lower volume of sales in the early months of the year when customers are trying to pay off their credit cards.

Keeping all that in mind, if you deduct from the monthly sales totals all your labor, materials, and overhead expenses, what's left is your net profit before taxes.

> **Tip...**
>
> **Smart Tip**
>
> Although paying by plastic is the popular trend, some of your customers will prefer to write you a check. Businesses lose more than $1 billion annually due to bad checks, so be sure to check several key items: accurate date; matching written and numerical amounts; and additional form of identification.

Couture and the Three Cs

Unlike some other entrepreneurs, one headache you won't have to deal with as an apparel store owner is worrying about when your customers will get around to paying you for your services. "Cash, check, or charge" are the three Cs you'll have to deal with in your business. The first two are easy. As for the third, unless you're setting up a funky stand on the Venice boardwalk in Southern California, most—if not all—of you will want to give your customers the option of paying by credit. That's the short and chic of it.

Two Things Are Certain: Clothes and Taxes

You're certainly with the majority of Americans if talking taxes makes you tense. And while taxes will never be the kind of experience equated with, say, buying a new pair of shoes, we at least hope you'll try our tips on for size.

Let's start with your business deductions. The more you have, the less you'll have to give to the government, though tax laws are constantly changing and soon, less may be more. In the apparel business you don't automatically get a deduction for purchasing inventory items for your business. Instead, you must reduce the amount paid for inventory purchases by the value of the inventory at the end of the year. For example,

The Tax Man Cometh

Businesses are required to pay a wide range of taxes, including conscientious clothing store owners. Keep good records so you can offset your local, state, and federal income taxes with the expenses of operating your company. Be sure you charge, collect, and remit appropriate sales tax on your products and services. If you have employees, you'll be responsible for payroll taxes. If you operate as a corporation, you'll have to pay payroll taxes for yourself; as a sole proprietor, you'll pay self-employment tax. Then there are property taxes, taxes on your equipment and inventory, fees and taxes to maintain your corporate status, your business license fee (which is really a tax), and other lesser-known taxes. This is when a really good accountant would come in handy.

if you paid $10,000 for merchandise in one year, and your inventory at the end of the year was $7,000, you could only deduct $3,000 for purchases in the year.

Nor will you have the luxury of writing off your store as you would a home office. You can deduct phone calls made from your store, clothing racks and other in-store fixtures, the cost of your business equipment and supplies, any subscriptions to fashion magazines and trade journals, and auto expenses, which count only when you drive in the course of "doing" or "seeking" business. This means meeting a rep at your local downtown apparel mart counts; hitting the local Saks for its spring sale does not.

You can also deduct entertainment and travel expenses for business purposes, like attending an apparel-related trade show or seminar, or even traveling to the far corners of the world to buy interesting fabric or accessories; travel expenses include airfare, bus or subway tickets, rental car mileage, hotels, and meals. (They do not include taking the family on a lavish summer vacation, during which you buy new school clothes for the kids.) We might remind you here that while it's kind of a pain, it's always wise to keep a log of your business miles, because it's even more of a pain to go back and guesstimate several months down the road, so to speak.

Other deductions that apply specifically to apparel entrepreneurs include any marketing or advertising that you do to promote your store, like that big grand opening we're so keen on, any pricey TV commercials that you create with a local ad agency, and any apparel-related trips that you're generous enough to offer as perks to your employees.

> **Beware!**
> Make sure that you open a separate business bank account for your apparel store. Commingling personal and professional funds can only lead to disaster.

> **Tip...**
>
> **Smart Tip**
> Depending on the size of your apparel store, you'll have to decide whether your volume warrants a full-time bookkeeper, an outside accountant, a year-end accounting and tax prep service—or any combination of the above.

Miscellaneous Record-Keeping

There are certain financial records unique to the apparel business that you'll need to keep. As an apparel store owner, you'll want to keep the following:

- *Sales records.* All income derived from the sale of your store's clothing and accessories can be grouped in one large category called gross sales, or into several subcategories for different product lines so that you know what merchandise is selling well and what's better off at your next garage sale.

- *Cash receipts.* These account for all money generated through cash sales and the collection of accounts receivable. This is actual income collected and doesn't include earnings from your sales records unless you choose to operate a cash-and-carry business. In a cash-and-carry business, your cash receipts theoretically match your sales records, and we can't imagine that will be the case with your apparel store.

- *Cash disbursements.* These are sometimes referred to as operating expense records or accounts payable. All disbursements should be made by check so that business expenses can be well documented for your accountant come tax time. If you make a cash payment to a manufacturer or a wholesaler, a receipt for the payment, or at least an explanation of it, should be included in your business records. As we've said, it is possible to obtain credit from your suppliers with very agreeable terms—officially referred to as trade credit—but it's also important not to abuse this. Never let accounts payable lapse beyond the terms. Also, breaking the cash disbursement headings into different categories, such as rent and advertising, may help simplify your records.

A petty cash fund should be established in cash disbursements to cover expenses that are immediate and small enough to warrant payment by cash, like dinner for your staff when they're working late or refreshments for that grand-opening bash. Record items purchased from the petty cash fund on a form that lists purchase date, amount, and purpose. When the petty cash fund is almost exhausted, total the cost of the items and write a check for the amount in order to replenish the account.

Oh No, Mr. Bill!

If your phone bill sometimes baffles you, try a vendor's invoice on for size. With regard to cash disbursements and accounts payable, almost all vendors' order forms read: Goods billed by the 25th of the month are due and payable by the 10th of the following month. The secret word here is "billed" because many vendors take the liberty of billing something on the 24th but don't actually send out the merchandise until the 28th or 29th. Check all your invoice dates against the actual UPS shipping date on the boxes. Under no circumstances is it acceptable for a vendor to invoice earlier than they ship.

Fun and Profit

There's a range of financial analyses you can use to determine the health of your business, but if this type of brain activity is enough to send you shopping, we'd recommend the less costly expedition of enlisting the help of an accountant. Again, the *Cliff's Notes* version is:

○ *Ratio analyses* offer a view into the competitive performance of your store in relation to similar apparel stores, like the store down the street and your local Gap.

○ *Measure of liquidity* is the amount of available liquid assets—otherwise known as available cash—your business has at any given time to meet accounts payable. (Hint: The more liquid you are, the better.)

○ *Current ratio* is the difference between your current assets and your current liabilities; all you need to have your accountant tell you here is a current ratio of assets to liabilities.

○ *Inventory turnover* is the number of times per year your inventory investment revolves.

○ *Asset earning power* is a ratio calculated by taking your earnings before taxes and interest and dividing that number by your total assets.

○ *Return on owner's equity* measures the return, or profit, you yield from the amount of equity you've invested in your business.

○ *Net profit on sales* measures the difference between your net sales and what you spend to operate your business. To determine the net profit on sales, you have to divide the net profit by the net sales.

○ *Investment turnover* is used to determine the amount of times per year that your total investment or assets revolve. To figure out turnover, divide your store's total annual net sales by your total assets.

○ *Return on investment (ROI)* determines the performance of a business based on its profitability. To figure out ROI, divide your store's net profit by total assets.

○ *Break-even analysis* is important when you're in the planning stages of your business. Essentially, the break-even analysis tells you how much you need to make—daily, weekly, or monthly—to pay all of your expenses by determining your monthly fixed and variable costs.

In addition, you will want to keep all records relating to major equipment purchases, like the purchase invoice and purchase date, vendor's name, a brief description of the item, how it was paid for, the check number, if appropriate, and the full amount of the purchase (so that you can deduct depreciation expenses come tax time), receiving reports, copies of sales slips, invoices sent to customers, canceled checks, and cash register tapes.

- *Insurance.* Keep all records pertaining to your store's insurance policies. This includes life, fire, and any special coverage you may obtain to decrease liability in a specific area. List the carriers of the policies, the underwriting agents who issued the coverages and the dates on which you wrote a check for the premium.

- *Advance deposits.* Many states require an advance deposit against future taxes to be collected. For example, in California, if you project $10,000 in taxable sales for the first three months of your store's operation, you must deposit 6.5 percent, in this case $650, with the state tax bureau when applying for your sales tax permit number.

- *Payroll.* If you employ more than one person in your store, you are required to withhold income tax and Social Security tax from each employee's paycheck and send these numbers to the proper tax collection agency. You will also need to obtain an employer tax number from the federal government using IRS form 1040 SS-4, and if your state has an income tax, from the state as well. You also have to maintain all records pertaining to payroll taxes (again, consult your accountant). As an employer, regardless of the number of employees you hire, you must maintain all records pertaining to payroll taxes (income tax withholding, Social Security and federal unemployment tax) for at least four years after the tax was due or paid, whichever is later.

Sample Income Statement

This annual income statement is based on a low-end hypothetical apparel store that we used as our start-up example in Chapter 8 with annual gross sales in the $200,000 range.

Fiona's Fashions
For the month of June 200x

Gross Sales for (month)	$16,770	
Less returns and allowances	− 310	
Net Sales		**$16,460**
Less Cost of Goods Sold		
Opening inventory, (month)	28,640	
Purchases during, (month)	3,810	
Freight charges	+ 75	
Total merchandise handled	32,525	
Less closing inventory, (month)	− 22,230	
Total Cost of Goods Sold		− $10,295
Gross Margin		**$6,165**
Operating Expenses		
Payroll	$2,195	
Rent	940	
Utilities	305	
Telephone	160	
Insurance	185	
Advertising	90	
Displays	150	
Depreciation	365	
Interest expense	60	
Delivery expense	210	
Stationery	75	
Travel and entertainment	60	
Dues and subscriptions	45	
Bad debts	80	
Miscellaneous	+ 110	
Total operating expenses		− $5,030
Operating Profit		**$1,135**
Other Income		
Dividends	35	
Interest on bank account	+ 60	
Total other income		+ 95
Total income before taxes		1,230
Less provision for income taxes		− 370
Net Profit		**$860**

Income Statement Worksheet

For the month of _____

Gross Sales for (month) _____

    Less returns and allowances _____

Net Sales _____

Less Cost of Goods Sold

    Opening inventory, (month) _____

    Purchases during, (month) _____

    Freight charges _____

      Total merchandise handled _____

      Less closing inventory, (month) _____

Total cost of goods sold _____

Gross Margin _____

Operating Expenses

    Payroll _____

    Rent _____

    Utilities _____

    Telephone _____

    Insurance _____

    Advertising _____

    Displays _____

    Depreciation _____

    Interest expense _____

    Delivery expense _____

    Stationery _____

    Travel and entertainment _____

    Dues and subscriptions _____

    Bad debts _____

    Miscellaneous _____

Total operating expenses _____

Operating Profit _____

Other Income

    Dividends _____

    Interest on bank account _____

Total other income _____

Total income before taxes _____

Less provision for income taxes _____

Net Profit _____

15

Tales from the
Front Lines

If you get nothing more from this business guide than the importance of money, location, and knowing your market's tastes, well, pat yourself on the back again, because you have learned the secret to success in the apparel business. It's not rocket science, but rather, as we have been saying all along, good business—and fashion—sense. With the

▲

right combination of these ingredients, plus smart buying, pricing, and advertising practices, you will be off to a healthy start.

Not to beat a dead horse, or maybe clothes horse would be more appropriate here, but whatever you do, heed the advice of our seasoned experts and entrepreneurs, including one who says, "The biggest problem facing small, independent apparel store owners is the mall. Chain store buyers can negotiate for better prices, and consumers can go to these stores and get whatever they need at better prices. What you need to do is make your store a preferred destination, whether that means an excellent location, great selection, friendly salespeople or, better yet, a combination of all three. You also need to make your store something special and unique."

Fashion Failures

We have tried to drive home the unique challenges of opening an apparel store, namely that fashion can be fickle in the same way that the restaurant business can be fickle. The long hours and sometimes long droughts when your apparel store may not be turning a profit are not for everyone. In fact, given the advice of everyone here, you can pretty much count on not making any money during your first year in business. We will also remind you that one of our entrepreneurs, Marcia Sauters, who owns a children's specialty shop in Santa Monica, has not turned a substantial profit in the 26 years she has been in business. Still, she can't imagine doing anything else.

"I'm surviving," she says. (Take notes here if you haven't already.) Sauters is surviving because she's followed some of the steps we've outlined in this business guide. She's changed locations when rents have gotten too high and the competition too close for comfort, and she's specialized her merchandise to differentiate herself from her competition and appeal to a broader customer base.

Since you've gotten this far, you have no doubt determined that you have more than just "good taste" in your personal business portfolio. We will again remind you of a big failure factor that we covered in Chapter 1: Having someone compliment you on your exquisite taste in clothes is not reason enough to start your own clothing store. It's only one good reason that should be supported by many others.

For any fledgling small-business owner, there are certain business basics you should be aware of and adhere to if you want your entrepreneurial endeavor to succeed. These are the obvious: sufficient working capital; keeping your spending and/or costs under control; maintaining good customer/client relations; coping with the competition; keeping adequate financial records; not overborrowing; and promoting and maintaining a favorable public image.

However, specific to the apparel business, you'll also need to avoid these fashion faux pas: ignorance of your buying market (opening Liberal Leisurewear in

Kennebunkport, Maine); not keeping abreast of market trends (leisure suits went out in the 1970s—and stayed out); overbuying/too much inventory; underpricing or over-pricing merchandise; employing surly salespeople/giving inadequate staff training (you can get that at any clothing store, along with better markdowns); bad supplier relations (an empty store really makes no profit); reluctance to seek the advice of experts (that's what friends are for); dated merchandising techniques; and renting store space that's too big (you can't take it with you).

Scared Solvent

We don't know how many ways we can say this, or how many ways our experts can drive this point home: Money will make the apparel entrepreneur's life much easier. If you do not have enough capital upfront, you may very well jeopardize the success of your business as well as the money you do invest. This is an overhead-intensive business. You've got a lot of working capital, inventory to buy and a store to furnish. We'll leave you with some testimonials:

"The biggest flaw in anyone's system is not being well-financed."
—*Waynette Davenport-Ford, owner of Davenport Designs in Savannah, Georgia*

"It helps if you have family for credit purposes and a fairly substantial amount of money."
—*K. Cohlmia, owner of The Wooden Nickel in Stillwater, Oklahoma*

"It may take you five years to break even."
—*Nancy Stanforth, Ph.D., Associate Professor, Kent State University's School of Fashion*

And finally, the parting words of D.L.S. Outfitters' president and owner Fred Derring:

"Successful small apparel stores are focused on the community, know their customers better, give terrific service, and have more interesting clothing on their floors."

Appendix
Clothing Store Resources

They say you can never be too rich or too young. While these could be argued, we believe "You can never have too many resources." Therefore, we present for your consideration a wealth of sources for you to check into, check out, and harness for your own personal information blitz.

These sources are tidbits, ideas to get you started on your research. They are by no means the only sources out there, and they should not be taken as the ultimate answer. We have done our research, but businesses do tend to move, change, fold, and expand. As we have repeatedly stressed, do your homework. Get out and start investigating.

As an additional tidbit to get you going, we strongly suggest the following: If you haven't yet joined the internet age, do it! Surfing the net is like waltzing through a library, with a breathtaking array of resources literally at your fingertips.

Associations

American Apparel and Footwear Association (AAFA), 1601 N. Kent St., Suite 1200, Arlington, VA 22209, (800) 520-2262, www.appareland footwear.org

Fashion Group International, Inc., 8 West 40th St., 7th Floor, New York, NY 10018, (212) 302-5511, www.fgi.org

International Association of Clothing Designers (IACD), 475 Park Ave., 17th floor, New York, NY 10016, (212) 685-6602

International Formalwear Association (IFA), 401 N. Michigan Ave., Chicago, IL 60611, (312) 321-5139, www.formalwear.org

National Association for Retail Marketing Services (NARMS), 2417 Post Rd., Stevens Point, WI 54481, (888) 52NARMS, www.narms.com

National Sporting Goods Association (NSGA), 1601 Feehanville Dr., Suite 300, Mt. Prospect, IL 60056, (800) 815-5422, www.nsga.org

Professional Apparel Association (PAA), 994 Old Eagle School Rd., Suite 1019, Wayne, PA 19087-1802, (800) 722-7712, www.proapparel.com

The National Register (publishes directories for the apparel industry), 110 East 9th St., #AL-19, Los Angeles, CA 90079, (213) 622-3601, www.thenationalregister.com

Textile/Clothing Technology Corporation, 211 Gregson Dr., Cary, NC 27511, (800) 786-9889, www.tc2.com

Books

The Apparel Industry, Richard Jones, Blackwell Publishing Limited

The Business of Fashion: Designing, Manufacturing, and Marketing, Leslie Davis Burns, Nancy O. Bryant, Fairchild Books & Visuals

Confessions of Shameless Self-Promoters, Debbie Allen, McGraw-Hill

Fashion Advertising and Promotion, Jay Diamond, Fairchild Books & Visuals

How to Start and Run Your Own Retail Business, Irving Bursteiner, Citadel Publishing

Online Shopper's Survival Guide, Jacquelyn Lynn, Entrepreneur Press

Retail in Detail, Ronald Bond, Entrepreneur Press

Secondhand Chic: Finding Fabulous Fashion at Consignment, Vintage, and Thrift Stores, Christa Weil, Pocket Books

Start and Run Your Own Shop: How to Open a Successful Retail Business, Val Clark, How-to-Books

Start Your Own Successful Retail Business, Entrepreneur Press and Gwen Moran, Entrepreneur Press

Valuable Vintage: The Insider's Guide to Identifying and Collecting Important Vintage Fashions, Elizabeth Mason, Three Rivers Press

What Mother Never Told Ya About Promotions: A Small Store Guide, T.J. Reid, Retail Resources Publications

What Mother Never Told Ya About Retail: A Small Store Survival Guide, T.J. Reid, Retail Resources Publications

Colleges Offering Fashion Merchandising Degrees

Berkeley College, White Plains, NY, (914) 694-1122

Brooks College, Long Beach, CA, (866) 746-5711

Kent State University, School of Fashion, Kent, OH, (330) 672-3000

Paris Fashion Institute, Boston, MA, (617) 268-0026

Parsons School of Design, New York, NY, (212) 229-8989

Ryerson Polytechnic University, Toronto, ON, Canada, (416) 979-5000

University of Rhode Island, Department of Textiles, Fashion Merchandising and Design, Kingston, RI, (401) 874-4574

Virginia Commonwealth University, Fashion Design & Merchandising, Richmond, VA, (804) 828-1699

West Valley College, Fashion Design and Apparel Technology, Saratoga, CA, (408) 867-2200

Consultants and Experts

Debbie Allen, Allen & Associates Consulting, Inc., PO Box 27946, Scottsdale, AZ 85255-0149, (800) 359-4544, www.debbieallen.com

Fred Derring/Lee Leonard, D.L.S. Outfitters, 44 W. 55th St., 2nd Fl., New York, NY 10019, www.discountfitters.com

T.J. Reid, P.O. Box 977, Armite, LA 70422, (800) 221-8615, www.tjreid.com

Nancy Stanforth, Ph.D., Associate Professor, Kent State University School of Fashion, Kent, OH, fashionschool.kent.edu

Fixture Suppliers

Baker Store Equipment (manufactures store fixtures and displays), Cleveland, OH, (216) 475-5900

Chromium Plating & Polishing Corp., Brooklyn, NY, (718) 387-9898

Fleetwood Fixtures (manufactures wooden & metal custom store fixtures, designs & displays), Reading, PA, (610) 779-7700

Hart, Schaffner and Marx (manufactures men's and boy's clothing), Chicago, IL, (312) 372-6300

Miller Mfg. Co. (manufactures displays and exhibits), Richmond, VA, (804) 232-4551

Nomadic Display (portable and custom modular exhibit systems), Alexandria, VA, (800) 732-9395, www.nomadicdisplay.com

Oxford Industries (manufactures men's & boy's clothing; women's swimwear), Atlanta, GA, (404) 659-2424, www.oxfordinc.com

Polyman Plastics Co. (manufactures display accessories, peg board hooks, strip hooks, and plastic furniture components), Waterloo, ON, (519) 747-0559

Total Plastics (Plastic sheets, rods, tubing, films, and fabricated parts), Kalamazoo, MI, (800) 231-0009, www.totalplastics.com

Major U.S. Merchandise Marts

AMC, Inc./AmericasMart, 240 Peachtree St. NW., #2200, Atlanta, GA 30303-1327, (404) 220-3000, www.americasmart.com

Charlotte Merchandise Mart, 2500 E. Independence Blvd., Charlotte, NC 28205, (704) 333-7709, www.carolinasmart.com

Dallas Market Center, 2100 Stemmons Fwy., 5th floor, Dallas, TX 75207, (214) 655-6100, www.dallasmarketcenter.com

Denver Merchandise Mart, 451 E. 58th St., #470, Rm. 2344, Denver, CO 80216, (303) 292-6278, www.denvermart.com

Giftcenter & Jewelry Mart, 888 Brannan St., San Francisco, CA 94103, (415) 861-7733, www.gcjm.com

International Home Furnishings Center, 210 E. Commerce St., High Point, NC 27260-5238, (336) 888-3700, www.ihfc.com

Indianapolis Gift Mart, 4475 Allisonville Rd., Indianapolis, IN 46205, (317) 546-0719

Kansas City Gift Mart, 6800 W. 115th St., Overland Park, KS 66211, (913) 491-6688

The L.A. Mart, 1933 S. Broadway, Los Angeles, CA 90007, (213) 749-7911

The Market Center, 230 Fifth Ave., New York, NY 10001, (212) 686-1203

The Merchandise Mart, Merchandise Mart Plaza, Suite 470, Chicago, IL 60654, (800) 677-6278, www.merchandisemart.com

Miami International Merchandise Mart, Radisson Centre, 777 NW 72nd Ave., Miami, FL 33126, (305) 261-2900

Minneapolis Gift Mart, 10301 Bren Rd. W., Minnetonka, MN 55343, (612) 932-7200, www.mplsgiftmart.com

The New York Merchandise Mart, 41 Madison Ave., New York, NY 10010, (212) 686-1203, www.41madison.com

Northeast Market Center, 1000 Technology Park Dr., Billerica, MA 01821, (978) 670-6363, www.thegiftcenter.com

Pittsburgh ExpoMart, 105 Mall Blvd., Monroeville, PA 15146, (412) 856-8100, www.pghexpomart.com

Seattle Gift Mart, 6100 4th Ave. S., Seattle, WA 98108, (206) 767-6800

Publications and Magazines

Apparel News, California Publications, 110 E. 9th St., Ste. A-777, Los Angeles, CA 90079, (213) 627-3737, www.apparelnews.net

The Apparel Strategist/The Apparel Statistical Review, PO Box 406, Fleetwood, PA 19522, (610) 944-8291, www.apparelstrategist.com

Big Beautiful Woman, Aeon Publishing (Ireland), (353) 16683856

Daily News Record, Fairchild Publications, 750 Third Ave., 10th Floor, New York, NY 10017, (800) 360-1700, www.dailynewsrecord.com

Earnshaw's Magazine, Symphony Publishing, 8 West 38th St., Suite 201, New York, NY 10018, (800) 731-5852, http://www.earnshaws.com/

Fashion International, Fashion Calendar Intl., 153 E. 87th St., New York, NY 10128, (212) 289-0420, www.fashioncalendar.net/international.htm

Footwear Plus Magazine, Symphony Publishing, 8 West 38th St., Suite 201, New York, NY 10018, (800) 731-5852, http://www.footwearplusmagazine.com

Brides, GQ, Glamour, Mademoiselle, Teen Vogue, Vanity Fair, Vogue, Condé Nast Publications, 350 Madison Ave., New York, NY 10017, (212) 880-8000, www.condenast.com

Seventeen, Hearst Magazines, 300 West 57th St., New York, NY 10019-3791, www.seventeen.com

Teen, Hearst Magazines, 300 West 57th St., New York, NY 10019-3791, www.teen mag.com

Visual Merchandising and Store Design, ST Publishing, 407 Gilbert Ave., Cincinnati, OH 45202, (513) 421-2050, www.stmediagroup.com

Women's Wear Daily, Fairchild Publications, (212) 630-4230, www.wwd.com

Successful Apparel Store Owners

K. Cohlmia, The Wooden Nickel, 225 S. Knoblock, Stillwater, OK 74074, www.shopthenickel.com

Waynette Davenport-Ford, Davenport Designs, 141 Bull St., Savannah, GA 31401, http://www.davenportdesigns.us, http://stores.ebay.com/Davenport-Designs

Richard and Bobigene Fent, The Secret Garden, 2420 W. Hwy. 76, Branson, MO 65616

Robert Loeb, Loeb's, 2209 Front St., Meridian, MS 39301, www.loebsclothing.com

Marcia Sauters, My New Friends, 1003 Broadway, Santa Monica, CA 90401, www.mynewfriends.com

Trade Shows and Meetings

Action Sports Retailer Show (ASR), 31910 Del Obispo, Suite200, San Juan Capistrano, CA 92675, (949) 226-5744, www.asrbiz.com

Apparel Clothing and Textile Industry Trade Shows Directory, www.apparelsearch.com/trade_show.htm

Biz Trade Shows for Apparel & Clothing, www.biztradeshows.com/apparel-fashion

Fashion Trade Shows Directory, http://tradeshow.alibaba.com/collection/Apparel.html

Imprinted Sportswear Shows, (800) 933-8735, www.issshows.com

Lingerie Americas, Inc., 525 Broadway, #702, New York, NY 10012, (212) 966-5830, www.lingerie-americas.com

MAGIC—Men's Apparel Guild in California, 6200 Canoga Ave., 2nd Floor, Woodland Hills, CA 91367, (818) 593-5000, www.magiconline.com

Outdoor Retailer Market, 31910 Del Obispo, Ste. 200, San Juan Capistrano, CA 92675, (949) 226-5722, www.outdoorretailer.com

Promotional Products Association International, 3125 Skyway Cir. N., Irving, TX 75038, (800) 426-7724, www.ppa.org

Sewn Products Industry Expo, 9650 Strickland Road, Suite 103-324, Raleigh, NC 27615, (919) 872-8909, www.spesaexpo.com

Specialty Graphic Imaging Association (SGIA), 10015 Main St., Fairfax, VA 22031-3489, (703) 385-1335, www.sgia.org

Specialty Trade Shows, www.spectrade.com

Glossary

"As is" goods: merchandise put out for sale, regardless of the condition.

Average markup: a composite of the relationship between all cost amounts and all retail amounts; in other words, the difference between what you pay a manufacturer and what you sell that merchandise for in your store.

Billed cost: the manufacturer's price for goods sold to a store.

Book inventory: value, at retail, of goods on hand.

Boutique: a shop designed to present specially selected merchandise (yes, this is more than likely you).

Buyer: the person—in the beginning, that may be you—responsible for choosing the merchandise that you'll sell in your store.

Cash discount: deduction from cost of goods for conformance to prearranged terms of payment; this is a completely above-board practice and, as you'll learn soon enough, something you acquire through polite negotiations with manufacturers.

Chain: a company that owns a group of stores; the Gap, for example, is a chain that owns Banana Republic and Old Navy.

▲

Clearance: the act of selling inventory at the end of the season in order to get rid of outdated stock.

Closeout: a group of goods offered at a reduced price by a resource to retailers at the end of the season.

COD: cash on delivery; again, as you'll learn, cash on hand is a powerful negotiating tool for discounts in this business.

Cost of goods: the total cost, including merchandise and freight charges.

Export: to carry or send goods to another country or countries for purposes of sale; Levi's jeans are a good example of one of this country's most famous exports.

Fashion: a style currently in vogue, generally associated with apparel and accessories.

Gross margin: the remainder after subtracting total cost of goods from retail amount of sales.

Import: to bring merchandise from another country for purposes of sale.

Initial markup: the difference between cost of goods and original retail price marked; your price markup may change as merchandise goes on sale.

Inventory: a term used to define stock and to actively count and record quantities of merchandise for the purpose of determining a dollar value of goods on hand.

Jobber: a middleman who purchases from the manufacturer and sells to the retailer.

Keystoning: the practice of doubling the wholesale cost to figure retail price; keystoning is very common in the apparel business.

Licensing: a contractual agreement and fee paid to the owner of an established product line by a company wishing to use/manufacture/sell the product and name of the line for a stated period of time. In this instance, a license will only be effective for a period of time, and unless exclusive, it does not stop the licensee from selling same license to other companies at the same time; once a license is up, the licensee has the right to decline or extend an agreement.

Merchandising: the part of marketing involved with promoting sales of merchandise by considering the most effective means of selecting, pricing, displaying, and advertising items for sale in a retail store.

OTB or open to buy: the dollar amount budgeted for inventory purchases for a given period (usually one, three, or four months).

Retail: the sale of goods to the ultimate consumer; when a customer comes into your store and buys an item off the rack, they're buying "retail" from you.

Sales rep: a person or company who represents the manufacturer and offers goods for sale to the retailer; a sales rep is different from a jobber in that he or she only represents certain manufacturers at certain times, while a jobber is more of a freelancer.

Shrinkage: the loss of merchandise at retail, caused by shoplifting, internal theft, or bookkeeping errors; you obviously want to keep shrinkage to a minimum.

SRP or suggested retail price: the price the manufacturer sets as the suggested selling price for you, the retailer, to pass on to the customer.

Terms: another word for the percentage the buyer has negotiated with the vendor.

Turnover: the number of times the average investment in merchandising is bought and sold during a given period; you obviously want to keep turnover at a maximum.

Vendor: the merchandise resource, also known as manufacturer.

Volume: the retail amount of goods sold during a given period, as in "sales volume."

Wholesale: the process of moving merchandise from the manufacturer to the retailer through the sales rep or jobber.

Index